THE FLINTSTONES®

From the beginning of time,

the world's greatest artists have searched for inspiration.

In their quests, many turned toward religion and the gods;

others honored nature.

But in the hearts and minds of an elite few

burned the desire to represent

a deeper and more meaningful subject.

—The Flintstones—

RENÉE MAGRANITE

ROY LIMESTONESTEIN

VINCENT VAN GARNET

HENROCK MATISSE

PABLO PIQUARTZO

KEITH HARRINGSTONE

JOAN MIRÓPAL

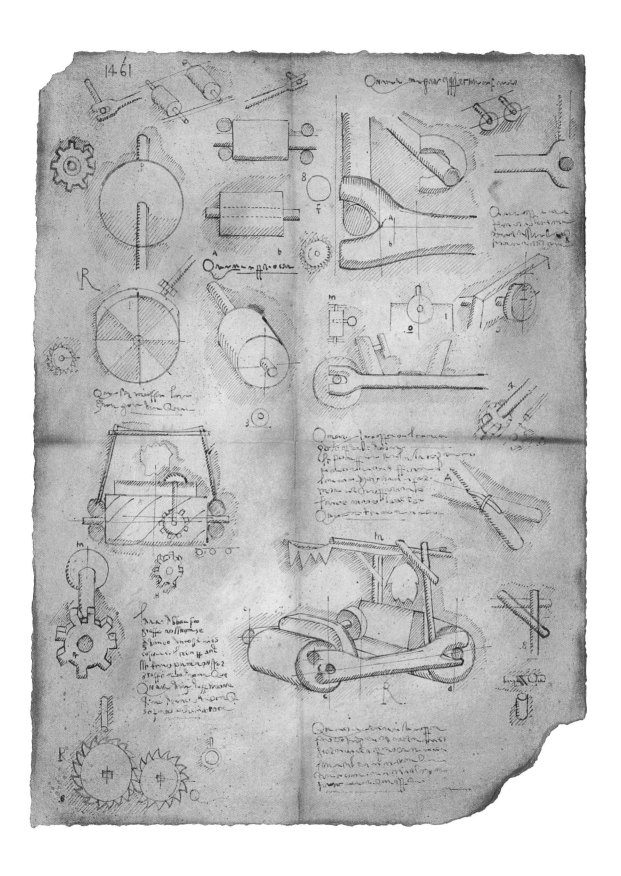

LEONARDO DA VINSHALE

SALVADOR DALIMITE

THIS BOOK IS DEDICATED TO

THE ANIMATORS, ARTISTS, VOICE ACTORS, WRITERS,

AND PRODUCTION PEOPLE—

PAST AND PRESENT—

WHOSE TALENTS BROUGHT "THE FLINTSTONES"

TO VIBRANT LIFE AND HAVE KEPT THEM LIVELY

THROUGH THE YEARS.

THE FLINTSTONES®

A Modern Stone Age Phenomenon

By T. R. Adams

MIRACLE PICTURES INC.

MIRACLE PICTURES
INC.
IF IT'S A GOOD PICTURE—
IT'S A MIRACLE

Turner Publishing, Inc.

ATLANTA

Library of Congress Cataloging-in-Publication Data

Adams, T. R.
    The Flintstones : a modern stone age phenomenon / by T. R. Adams. —
    1st ed.
      p.   cm.
    Includes index.
    ISBN 1-57036-012-X : $29.95
    1. Flintstones (Television program) I. Title.
    PN1992.77.F59A3 1994
791.45'72—dc20   94-20670
                                                        CIP

Published by Turner Publishing, Inc.
A Subsidiary of Turner Broadcasting System, Inc.
1050 Techwood Drive, N.W.
Atlanta, Georgia 30318

Distributed by Andrews and McMeel
A Universal Press Syndicate Company
4900 Main Street
Kansas City, Missouri 64112

Editor—Crawford Barnett
Copy Editor—Lauren Emerson
Art Director—Michael Walsh
Designer—Robert Zides
Gallery Paintings—Phillip Brooker
Picture Editor—Marty Moore
Picture Research—Tom Wogatzke

First Edition 10 9 8 7 6 5 4 3 2 1

Printed in the U.S.A.

(previous page)
**The opening scene
from episode P–14,
"The Monster From
the Tar Pits."**

CONTENTS

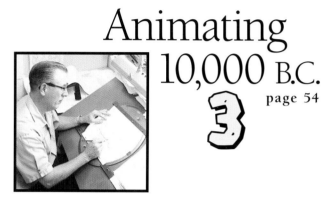

CHAPTER ONE

The Creation

"Yabba-Dabba-Doo!" With the shriek of a whistle the workday is over, and a Modern Stone Age quarry worker dashes home, his exuberant cheer ringing from television sets around the world. Audiences everywhere recognize the voice; it belongs to none other than that boisterous and brash prehistoric everyman, Fred Flintstone. Fred; his wife, Wilma; and their neighbors, Betty and Barney Rubble; have delighted television viewers since they first drove down the streets of Bedrock (courtesy of Fred's two feet) and over the airwaves on September 30, 1960. With that first broadcast "The Flintstones" became landmark television, the first ever prime-time animated series, and a phenomenon was born. Through the magic of cable, broadcast, and satellite television, Bedrock exists all over the world. Its denizens speak twenty-two languages in more than eighty countries, and can be seen some-where any hour of the day or night. Having starred in full-length feature films as well as a score of television series and

specials, "The Flintstones" have earned a place in entertainment history. But like most Hollyrock legends, they started out in relative obscurity, their names known to only a few.

In fact, like Marilyn Monroe, Cary Grant, and a host of other stars, their original names were changed by the studio. But then, that's getting ahead of the story.

The casting call went out when John Mitchell of Screen Gems, an influential entity in the television production world and the distributor for Hanna-Barbera Productions, suggested a prime-time animated series.

Because family-based situation comedies were currently popular, the Hanna-Barbera artists went to work developing happy broods. A crowd of contemporary moms and pops, along with their offspring and pets, were created, considered, and rejected, including a host of back-to-the-land types: farmers, hillbillies, and even gypsies. Nothing clicked. They all lacked the charisma that William Hanna and Joseph Barbera, the company's founders, were looking for, so the artists began moving backward in time, to cowboys, Pilgrims, and ultimately Romans. But none of the ideas had star quality. . . .

Finally Dan Gordon, a storyboard illustrator, was struck with a bolt of cartoon genius and sketched two characters in animal skins and a bird with a long beak playing a stone record. "When you saw the bird playing the phonograph record, you could immediately think of other gags like the elephant's trunk for washing the car or watering the flowers, birds' beaks for clothespins," Bill Hanna recalls. A modern couple sitting in a modern car had no spark, but put them in animal skins, sitting in a skin-topped convertible with stone rollers for wheels, and the laugh was there. An average guy—coincidentally wearing a leopard

Studio press releases have always described the Flintstone home as a "split-level cave," as seen in this early pencil sketch (opposite, top). Although the chimney is usually present (right), the fireplace shown in the sketch of the living room (opposite, middle), like so many of the home's amenities, is not a permanent fixture and appears only when written into the script. An early rendering of a Modern Stone Age Bedroom (opposite, bottom).

"When you saw
the bird playing
the phonograph,
you could immediately
think of other gags.**"**

—Bill Hanna

tunic—pounding away at a stone piano, the lady of the house answering a ram's horn telephone, a lawn mower fashioned from a crab on wheels, all suggested more and more ideas.

Dan Gordon's sketches were sent to Ed Benedict, who molded them into the Fred, Wilma, Betty, and Barney we all recognize today. A gifted artist who had worked on Hanna-Barbera's first made-for-television cartoon series, "Ruff and Reddy," Benedict endowed his subjects with a delightful simplicity. Besides acting as make-over consultant, Benedict also wore the hat of set designer, establishing the stylistic tone for Bedrock's playfully cockeyed Modern Stone Age architecture.

Situated two hundred and fifty feet below sea level, in the seat of Cobblestone County, Bedrock might be called the first master-planned community. An aerial view of this city of 2,500 was drawn to guide animators and layout artists around the town, which included a supermarket, restaurants, a drive-in theater, and, of course, a bowling alley. The completed town was then christened Bedrock; its first family, the Flagstones.

With the concept agreed upon, Joe Barbera and Dan Gordon outlined two simple stories: in one, Fred and Barney attempt to share ownership of a backyard swimming pool; the other involves a plot the two friends devise to get out of having to attend the opera with their wives. These plots later became the basis for shows P–1, "The Swimming Pool," and P–2, "The Flintstone Flyer."

BARNEY-BETTY-BEDROOM

Gordon drew up the storyboards. In animation, key scenes are normally drawn in comic-strip format, nine frames on a sheet of paper. These storyboards, however, were individual four-by-five-inch sketches, one to a page. Numbering about four hundred, they papered three walls of a room. And to complete the decor, there were larger pieces of art set on easels against the fourth wall.

In early 1960, with all this artwork in tow, Barbera began what would become a marathon effort—attempting to sell the show to television networks and ad agencies. Accompanied by John Mitchell, Hanna-Barbera's Screen Gems agent, he flew to New York and checked into a room at the Sherry Netherland, which would become his home for eight long weeks.

Who Put the Spark in The Flintstones?

Ed Benedict has been a well-kept secret for many years. He's the artist who gave the early Hanna-Barbera cartoons their distinctive look by designing from scratch most of the studio's classic characters. Surprisingly, Benedict says that there was nothing special or "romantic" about his work as a freelance artist. In fact, he's amused that anyone would be interested in his past creations. To him "The Flintstones" was just another assignment. He attached no sentimentality to Fred and Wilma—characters he sketched in the dining room of his Cheviot Hills home in west Los Angeles.

As he recalls, there were few formal parameters provided for the cave people. "I got the assignment [from Joe Barbera] and went home to scribble. I'd walk away from it, go out in the garage and saw wood, and come back and monkey around with it some more. It certainly didn't seem monumental." In fact, the success and longevity of "The Flintstones" is an amazement to the man who created their likenesses.

Benedict's assignment from Hanna-Barbera included a new look. "The studio," Benedict says, "wanted to get away from that round, roly-poly, Micky-Mousie kind of thing. Less smooth. Something more contemporary . . . I don't think the animators liked me too much because they weren't accustomed to drawing the characters I designed." After Benedict gave the show its "rocky" edge and a Modern Stone Age semblance, Hanna-Barbera ran with his designs. "Joe was smart," says Benedict. "I would have preferred the more crude caveman, but he brought me down to earth. They refined them, making the drawings more commercial." Laying no claim to the show's tremendous success, Benedict remarks, "I didn't make 'The Flintstones' popular. Commerce made them popular. Hanna-Barbera made them popular. But," he says hesitatingly, "the characters *have* lasted."

LEAN BACKWARDS FOR MOST RUNS

Ed Benedict's sketches depict early ideas for the Flintstones and Rubbles. Some characteristics carried over to the final versions, such as Barney's big nose and the fact that Fred is always the taller of the two friends. Betty and Wilma have retained their feminine figures, although they are now portrayed in a less seductive manner.

Using Screen Gems' Manhattan office as a base, Barbera pitched the series daily, giving hour-and-a-half, one-man shows in which he acted out all the voices, sound effects, and gags. Sometimes he did the show four and five times a day. But with the repetition Barbera learned how to play the audience. "As you kept doing it, you knew where to look for your laughs, you knew what sound effects to make, you knew where to hit a punch here and there to hit some gag."

He perfected his routine, and the word on Madison Avenue was that his act was the one to catch. And although "The Flagstones" had no buyer, it was getting some great laughs. On one occasion, however, while playing to a packed house, Barbera inexplicably got no reaction at all. Worried that he had lost his touch, he discovered the reason at the end of the show. Two rival advertising agencies were present, and neither wanted to tip off the other by appearing to enjoy the pitch.

Another time Barbera ran through the show for the entire staff of a well-known pharmaceutical firm. Just as he arrived back at his hotel, exhausted, they called him on the phone. "The president of the company couldn't make it, but he's here now. Do you think you could do it over again?" "Sure," Barbera croaked as he headed for the door.

After each performance the reaction was always the same: Everybody loved the show, but no one wanted to commit to anything as radical as a prime-time animated series. "It's the only fresh thing we've seen for television in many seasons," one executive told Barbera just before rejecting the proposal. Cartoons were considered strictly kiddie fare, and stretching one to an entire half hour was unheard of.

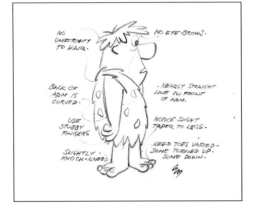

"At least there's no blood and guts running in the streets."

—R. J. Reynolds executive

Early poses of Fred gave him a rough appeal and a befuddled visage. Ed Benedict, who drew the sketches, was not unfamiliar with cavemen, having designed the characters for the 1955 Tex Avery MGM cartoon, "The First Bad Man."

After eight weeks of unrelenting rejection, Joe was almost ready to admit defeat. But he had one network left to pitch, and he wasn't going to quit until he had exhausted every option. Only then would he go home.

Joe began his presentation at nine o'clock sharp. At nine-fifteen—Barbera remembers the time as clearly as he does the birth of his first child—ABC bought the show. The network had already proven itself innovative through strategies such as purchases of theatrical movies for television, and in March 1960, it took another imaginative—if seemingly chancy—step.

Barbera was thrilled to return to California, the endless nightmare of performances behind him. But no sooner had he arrived at home and collapsed exhausted on the bed than the phone rang. Bad news. He had to return to New York and do the show all over again. Ad time still hadn't been sold, and Screen Gems felt that he was the only one who could do the job.

Reestablished in the Big Apple, Barbera took a train to Winston-Salem, North Carolina, to the corporate offices of the R. J. Reynolds Tobacco Company. Upon arrival he was shown into the conference room, a lavish chamber richly paneled in fine hardwoods.

Feeling it would be criminal to use the push pins he normally employed to hold up his drawings, Barbera carefully and laboriously affixed each sketch with one small, unobtrusive piece of tape.

SOMETIMES -
USE HAIR FOR
ACTION -

SLIGHT
LEAN
BACK FOR
MOST RUNS.

WHEN POSSIBLE.
USE A NEARLY
STRAIGHT LINE
TO RELIEVE A
CURVED LINE -
AS ON LEGS, ARMS.

L ike the most complicated, screwball plot of a "Flintstones" episode, the story of who actually came up with the concept for the show is fraught with misconceptions and disagreements. Trying to unravel all the threads would require all the skills of prehistoric detective Perry Gunite, and even that ace gumshoe would have to admit that in many creative efforts there is no one idea architect; concepts often fall into place from many sources and minds.

Jerry Eisenberg, a Hanna-Barbera layout artist, believes that his father, Harvey, came up with the "seed concept" for the show. A former MGM animator and freelance comic book artist, the senior Eisenberg had known Bill Hanna and Joe Barbera for years. As Jerry tells it, Harvey pitched the cave-person angle to Barbera during a lunch and subsequently told his son, "I think I've just given Joe Barbera a pretty good idea for nothing." Years later, Alan Dinehart, a "Flintstones" writer, overheard Jerry discussing his father's role in the show and clarified the story: "Your father walks into the room and we all have our sketches of 'The Honeymooners' laid out on the table. They were sketches of Jackie Gleason, Art Carney, and the two gals. He looks at them and says, 'Why not put some skins on 'em and put them in the prehistoric ages?'"

Milt Rosen, a television comedy writer, has a different tale: "I got called in by Joe Barbera at their little offices at Chaplin Studios, which is now A&M Records. They were looking for a show to go with a drawing they had of cavemen. The studio gave me five hundred dollars to come up with something, but my head wasn't really with it because I was going through a divorce. The best I could do after a few weeks was come up with 'The Honeymooners' in animation. And I came up with the name Rubble. Those were mine."

Bill Hanna acknowledges the differing points of view over the concept's origin. "Now, you may not get the same response from anybody else," he says, "but to me, Dan Gordon is responsible for 'The Flintstones.' He came up with the basic concept of doing it with cavemen, in skins."

Apparently, "The Flintstones" was a good idea whose time had come. Preston Blair, formerly of Disney fame, submitted treatments for an animated "Honeymooners" to studios around Hollywood. And a cartoon Stone Age? It had been around for years. Gertie, an animated dinosaur, came to life in 1914, and "Ally Oop," a comic strip featuring cavemen, was going strong in the thirties. Even artist Ed Benedict, the man who was hired to style the Flintstone characters, designed cave people for the 1955 MGM Tex Avery cartoon, "The First Bad Man." But "The Flintstones" was unique; the Hanna-Barbera team took a seedling of an idea and nurtured it until it grew into a phenomenon.

The leaning bodies depicted in the Ed Benedict sketch above are representative of classic Hanna-Barbera style.

Early design ideas for Barney (below). "We'd worked with MGM on cartoons of humans," Bill Hanna says, "so doing them for 'The Flintstones' wasn't a major transition. We also used very contemporary situations, which helped to maximize the comedy."

His preparations complete, he went downstairs for a quick cup of coffee. Returning to the conference room, Joe opened the door and discovered to his horror that all the drawings had fallen off the walls. With his audience due any minute, he rushed around the room in a frenzy, this time using two large pieces of tape to secure the drawings.

No sooner had he finished than the company president came in, accompanied by several corporate executives. Shortly thereafter, Bowman Gray, the chairman of the board, entered, moving slowly and painfully with the help of a cane. Barbera went into his pitch, explaining that it was necessary for his audience to stand at his back to best view the sketches. Despite the discomfort he was obviously in, Gray politely complied, following Joe from one line of sketches to the next. Because of the pain Gray didn't so much as crack a smile. And his executives, not wanting to differ from their boss, remained stone-faced as well. Barbera wrote the whole thing off as a disaster. But to his surprise, they bought the show. "At least there's no blood and guts running in the streets," they said by way of acceptance.

The campaign was not over yet, because R. J. Reynolds had purchased only half of the show's commercial time. Barbera's next trip was to Chicago to pitch the Miles Laboratory people. Arriving at two o'clock in the morning, he went directly to the conference room and began pinning up his sketches. Finishing with barely time for a nap, he was back at eight for the big sell. And once again he succeeded. They bought the show, and to this day are still manufacturing Flintstones Vitamins for children.

With a network and sponsors for his prehistoric progeny, Barbera returned triumphantly to Hollywood. His euphoria, however, was short-lived. Problems seemed to assault the project from all sides. Having agreed to do the show, the network wanted product fast, and the Hanna-Barbera team was forced to work under a strict time deadline. Unfortunately, output was restricted by the fact that advertising agencies were utilizing the

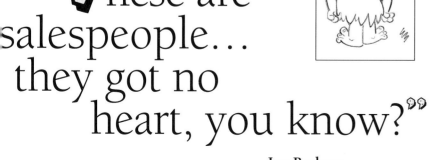

"These are salespeople... they got no heart, you know?"

—Joe Barbera

In the concept sketches at left, Joe Barbera circled in red the individual features that he preferred and the final result was Betty Rubble, almost as she appears today.

skills of professional animators for television commercials and their services were in high demand. "Everybody was working outside," Dick Bickenbach, the show's layout artist, remembers. "All the animators picked up at night; five o'clock came and they were working for someone else."

Several weeks after the show had been sold, Barbera recalls with a laugh, Hanna confronted him with bleak news. Given their current production flow, there was no way they could deliver "The Flagstones" in time to meet the September deadline imposed by the network. The partners agreed that Hanna would call Screen Gems and gracefully bow out.

"Sparks came out of the phone," Barbera relates. "Smoke and fire and brimstone came out of the phone." Jerry Hyams, the president of the company, was not happy. Threatening to sue Hanna-Barbera for every penny they had, Hyams yelled into the mouthpiece, "You cannot do this to us."

At eight the next morning, Bill and Joe were assaulted by a horde of fire-breathing Screen Gems representatives who had commandeered a red-eye from New York. "What do you got? Show me what you got there," they barked. "These are salespeople," Barbera remarks, "they got no heart, you know? . . . So finally they looked at a few feet of film that we'd shot and," he growls, "they wanted the end of the show."

The fact that the dragons liked what they saw enough to want the rest provided the shot in the arm that Hanna and Barbera needed, and they set back to work at a feverish pace. With the team burning the creative candle at both ends and using every animator's trick they knew to cut production time, the show neared completion.

The details needed for the series seemed legion, and so the studio launched into a program of prehistoric research, examining the flora, fauna, and habitats of

Shortly before "The Flintstones" made its network premiere, ABC issued a press release that described the show, included visuals of the main characters (below), detailed the prior successes of Screen Gems and Hanna-Barbera, and emphasized the ideal time slot that the series was positioned in—from 8:30 to 9:00 every Friday evening. This placed it between the "upbeat new half-hour family series, 'Harrigan & Son' . . . and one of the strongest shows in all television, '77 Sunset Strip'." Junior, the little boy on the cover of the press release—drawn by Ed Benedict (facing page)—made only one other appearance, in a very early Little Golden Book Flintstones adventure.

Only weeks before the first episode went on the air, the show's name had to be changed.

MEET THE FLINTSTONES

ABC-TV SALES DEVELOPMENT DEPT.

Rare footage was recently unearthed from Hanna-Barbera's film storage facility in Kansas City where the original Screen Gems library had been stored in disarray since the 1960s: a minute-and-42-second "screen test" of "The Flagstones" that was made shortly before the name change to Flintstone. Having disappeared into legend for thirty-four years, this clip was first used to assuage financial backers who wanted to see how their money was being spent, and later to show potential advertisers the cartoon. As with the early work of so many Hollyrock notables, the Flintstones and the Rubbles appear unrefined, even coarse, yet they still exhibit that flicker of future greatness.

The scene opens on the Rubbles' house, a rounded stone edifice with Betty framed in the window. But this is not the Betty Rubble we remember. She is pale pink, with black dot eyes, a pencil curve of a mouth (she wears no lipstick—in fact, she has no lips), and a mop of black hair that looks exactly like . . . well, a kitchen mop, right down to the little knot on top.

And the scene becomes stranger still when the rest of the cast appears. Wilma displays her characteristic wry attitude when she tells Betty that she can go shopping "as soon as I serve his majesty's lunch," yet to look at her, she is barely recognizable. Her famous red hair is sandy blond and her skin is bone white. Fred and Barney appear almost surrealistic. Each is darkly tanned with lavender stubble. Barney, on his way to go spear fishing in Fred's pool, is wearing a diving mask, his gargantuan nose protruding from its center. Fred is reclining lazily on an animal skin raft, about to eat the lunch that Wilma has prepared for him. The clip ends when Barney accidentally punctures the raft and Fred comments, "Barney, boy, you're making it tough to be friends." Always practical, Barney smiles cheerfully and says, "No use in wasting a lunch," taking the platter of food just as the big man submerges.

This screen test formed the basis for show P-1, "The Swimming Pool"—the very first episode to be produced—and although the characters' odd colorations are gone, animation in this episode still retains a rough quality that was smoothed out in subsequent shows.

Stone Age Screen Test

the period. Then the artists added their own special twists. A sketch of a realistic object combined with a spate of "goofing up," and a Modern Stone Age item emerged.

Dick Bickenbach speaks of creating Bedrock devices with an offhand ease. "Joe would say, 'we want a cuckoo clock,' and so I'd make one and take it in to him." But it wasn't always quite that simple. In creating a monster, the artists drew a dozen different models before hitting on the right formula. The rejected models were carefully filed away for future reference. And in this manner, many creations could emerge from the same initial concept.

Mildred, Fred's dino-crane at the quarry, exemplifies this creative progression: draw ridges on her back, change her expression a little, and she's the stairway at the Macyrock Department Store. Shrink her down, shorten her front legs and neck, change her color to grape, and you've got Dino, the Flintstones' lovable pet.

While the artists were playing Dr. Frankenstein, Hoyt Curtin, the show's musical director, was busy in his own laboratory composing a theme song and working out musical punches to accentuate Hanna and Barbera's animated schtick. The gags themselves could be anything from Fred and Barney getting rolled up in wallpaper to Barney rolling downhill, through town, and onto the freeway in a baby buggy.

"I remember one of the first episodes," Jean Vander Pyl, the voice of Wilma, says, "where Fred comes out to the front yard and Arnold the newsboy calls out, 'Here's your paper!' and tosses out a huge stone slab that knocks Fred over. And Fred says, 'I hate the Sunday paper.' Adults must have howled when they saw that—they *knew* what Sunday papers were like—kids just liked his getting knocked over." The show was the perfect mixture of satire, slapstick, and distinct personalities. "Husbands and wives could watch the show," says

The cast of the cartoon—still titled "The Flagstones"—as they appeared shortly before making their television debut. Although Ed Benedict created the characters, they were subtly refined through the work of the various artists who animated them. "It's hard for any one person to point to a cartoon and say, 'That's mine,'" Iwao Takamoto, the studio's creative director, explains. "Most animated characters are a composite of many people's work."

S eated behind his Stoneway piano, Hoyt Curtin groans when he thinks of the frantic schedules he used to keep as musical director of Hanna-Barbera. "In one year we had nine shows going. Nine shows! That was a back-breaking workload. Luckily, we had some of the best studio musicians in town. It was pure sight reading of some complicated pieces, with heavy time limits. But believe me, these guys were readin' demons!" Curtin, who composed the music for the Academy Award-winning *Magoo Flew* and the Emmy Award-winning "Huckleberry Hound," is something of a demon himself—at least in terms of productivity. In all, he has composed, arranged, and conducted music and titles for nearly three hundred Hanna-Barbera productions.

A fixture at Hanna-Barbera since the studio's inception, Curtin began his musical career at UPA, scoring the Mr. Magoo theatrical shorts. He also composed music for a variety of feature films and TV commercials, and in fact met Hanna and Barbera at MGM when the three collaborated on a commercial.

Now retired from the studio, Curtin is a legend not only at Hanna-Barbera; he has been hailed as a master in the cartoon music field. "He was an incredible craftsman," says cartoonist Mike Kazaleh, "The music he did was not only well written but designed in such a way that if you cut it into bits and pieces and rearranged them, they would still flow. That's planning."

Maestro of the Flints-Tunes

"Hoyt was a genius arranger," elaborates Jordan Reicheck, an animation designer. "What really created a chemical reaction between him and Hanna-Barbera was that he was able to arrange music in such a way that it made up for the lack of animation. . . . What really fills in the gaps is Hoyt's arrangements and what he does with the sound effects."

In addition to the studio's other projects, Curtin was responsible for the theme and background music for every episode of "The Flintstones." It was an especially challenging project because, as Curtin explains, "cartoon people don't offer the same hand and body movements, for shading and emphasis, which are available with humans." The soundtrack was used to counter much of this, and from beginning to end each episode used music to highlight the action and punch up the gags. Curtin chose the bass clarinet to represent Fred and Barney; woodwinds for Wilma and Betty. "Bill and Joe just let me go!" he said, adding that while they would comment on his work, they never told him they didn't like the way he had put something together.

Sometimes when they were brainstorming over the phone, Hanna and Barbera would come up with lyrics, and Curtin would be asked to create the music. "I'd literally sing the music . . . practically off the top of my head. That's how we did quite a few of our main themes, right over the telephone."

Early model sheets for "The Gladstones," one of the early names for the series. Note on the page for Fred, the hand correction reflecting the name change to Flintstone.

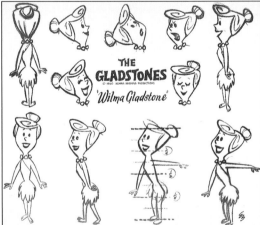

Vander Pyl, "and turn to each other and say, 'That's just what you do!'"

But there were some major last-minute changes before, as Joe Barbera puts it, "the magic happened." Only weeks before the first episode went on the air, the show's name had to be changed. The surname of the "Hi and Lois" comic strip characters was Flagston, uncomfortably close to Fred and Wilma's moniker. For "about ten minutes," Joe Barbera recalls, the Stone Agers existed as the Gladstones, and then someone at Screen Gems suggested the Flintstones. "We thought that was bad," Dick Bickenbach recalls, "because it would be stingy, like a skinflint." Today it's hard to imagine Fred and Wilma being called anything else, but then who can imagine Cary Grant as Archibald Leach?

And the problems continued. "The guys we recorded for five shows sounded okay at

A gifted animator, character designer, and storyboard artist, Dan Gordon "was almost mythical in his abilities," says Buzz Potamkin, an executive producer at Hanna-Barbera. "He could draw better than just about anybody on the face of the earth." "He was a key artist at MGM," adds Bill Hanna, noting that Gordon began working at Hanna-Barbera "as soon as we started to be Hanna-Barbera. He worked on 'Ruff and Reddy,' 'Huckleberrry Hound,' and all those early productions. He storyboarded 'The Flintstones' and was with us until he passed away."

Gordon brought a wealth of cartoon experience with him when he started at Hanna-Barbera. He had worked at Terrytoons, at Fleischer—coincidentally on a number of Stone Age cartoons—and also was well known in comic book circles for his contributions to the "Ha Ha" and "Giggles" titles.

"His style is hard to describe," says Jerry Beck, an animation producer and researcher, "but it had a looseness and also a solidity. The characters were so expressive. Dan had a gutsy style and was very frank in his writing. . . . He showed you how people really acted." Gordon's influence is evident in "The Flintstones" in the way they express the foibles of real people in all their nuances, from Fred's brash arrogance to his underlying warmth—with that all-important goofiness thrown in to make the stories funny.

"The best 'Flintstones' episodes," explains Jordan Reicheck, an animation designer, "are the ones with Dan's touches. He put more cartooniness in than anyone else. . . . The first season contains the best stuff because Dan Gordon had so much to do with it. To me," he adds, "Dan Gordon and Ed Benedict are the two people who made Hanna-Barbera what it is."

"Dan was the standard we all tried to match," says Tony Benedict, a studio writer and animator during the "Flintstones" days. "He was one of those people who could do everything. Joe

could describe something to him and Dan would start illustrating and these beautiful drawings would come out."

Gordon was also gifted with "an incredible sense of humor," Benedict says, "and it went on all the time; he never seemed to be down about anything. He loved to do jokes about Joe. For example, Joe has a lot of hair on his body and Dan used to call him 'The Tarantula.' " Remembered for his draftsmanship and mechanical drawing skills, as well as his wild sense of humor, Gordon's abilities are still used as a yardstick for studio excellence.

Like most towns, Hollyrock has its share of gossip mills, and a favorite topic of discussion is the idea that "The Flintstones" was based on "The Honeymooners," a Fifties sitcom about a loud-mouthed, overweight bus driver, his harried spouse, and their dim-witted but good-natured neighbor and his wife.

Fueling this gossip, though, was the rumor that Jackie Gleason, the spirit behind "The Honeymooners," at one time wanted to sue Hanna-Barbera for imitating his program. In fact, as Henry Corden, a friend of Gleason's and the second voice of Fred Flintstone, recalls, "Jackie's lawyers told him he could probably have 'The Flintstones' pulled right off the air. But they also told him, 'Do you want to be known as the guy who yanked Fred Flintstone off the air? The guy who took away a show that so many kids love, and so many of their parents love, too?' And apparently Jackie thought it over and decided against it."

But is the gossip true? Was the concept borrowed from "The Honeymooners"? "At that time 'The Honeymooners' was the most popular show on the air," explains Bill Hanna, "and for my bill, it was the funniest show on the air. The characters, I thought, were terrific. Now, that influenced greatly what we did with 'The Flintstones.'" As further clarification, he adds, "'The Honeymooners' was there, and we used that as a kind of basis for the concept."

The Great Honeymooners Controversy

"I don't remember mentioning 'The Honeymooners' when I sold the show," Barbera says, "but if people want to compare 'The Flintstones' to 'The Honeymooners,' then great. It's a total compliment. 'The Honeymooners' was one of the greatest shows ever written."

rehearsal," Barbera says. "But I'm going through the shows and I'm listening to the tracks and I know damned well something's wrong. This is where you get fooled. In testing, their voices sounded okay; in the shows, death." The voices just didn't work well once they were married to the animation. He quickly recast them, giving the part of Fred to Alan Reed and the part of Barney to Mel Blanc, and the show was transformed.

Barbera's instincts could not have been more accurate. Alan Reed wasn't just the voice of Fred, he *was* Fred Flintstone. In fact, it was Alan who came up with Fred's famous cheer. "In a recording session," Barbera reminisces, "Alan said, 'Hey, Joe, where it says yahoo, can I say yabba-dabba-doo?' I said yeah. God knows where he got it, but it was one of those terrific phrases." According to Alan, he got the idea from his mother, who used to say, "a little dab'll do ya," something she probably borrowed from a Brylcreem commercial.

From off-the-cuff improvisations to long hours of arduous work, "The Flintstones" became a reality, and, over the years, an animated entertainment classic in which Fred's gleeful shout still resounds after more than three decades.

"Hey, Joe, where it says yahoo, can I say yabba-dabba-doo?"

—**Alan Reed**

Fred gives his famous cheer in an animator's pencil sketch (below, left). The drawing is from a later period in the Flintstones' history, as evidenced by Fred's smoother, less primitive appearance.

The script from "The Flintstone Flyer" episode with Alan Reed's change from "yahoo" to "yabba-dabba-doo" penciled in (below).

IT WORKS
HE'S REALLY FLYIN'
HEY BARNEY!! (3) *Barney B*
BARNEY: WHAT DO YOU SAY NOW, FREDDIE
FRED: WHAT DO I SAY?
   YAHOO! *dabadoo*
   WE DID IT, WE'RE A SUCCESS!
BARNEY: WE???
FRED: RIGHT BARNEY BOY
   WITH MY BRAINS AND YOUR ER-A-
   A FORTUNE!
   THINK OF IT!

CHAPTER TWO

Before Bedrock

Bill Hanna and Joe Barbera, two names that are almost as well-known as Fred and Barney, are the creative spirits behind Bedrock and countless other celluloid worlds. Although their names have been synonymous with cartoons for over fifty years, neither man began his career with animation aspirations. Bill Hanna was born in Melrose, New Mexico, on July 14, 1910. Shortly after he began school, his family moved to California and Hanna took up the saxophone. Although it was a seemingly insignificant event at the time, the musical skill he acquired would later prove to be essential in advancing his animation career. But at the time, cartoons were still far in Hanna's unforeseen future, and in junior college, his focus was on a dual track of journalism and engineering. Then, in 1929, with the crash of the stock market, his studies came to a sudden halt, and he hit the streets looking for work. He was lucky; he landed a job

A writer and animator who worked on many "Flintstones" episodes, Tony Benedict also penned wickedly funny sketches of his bosses. "Bill and Joe," he says, when asked how the two took his pen-and-ink ribbing, "were torn because they liked the humor, but they didn't like being ribbed." They did, however, appreciate the fact that Benedict's sketches not only helped enliven and lighten the always heavy workload, but also demonstrated that creativity was appreciated in all its forms (facing page).

working on the construction of the Pantages Theater, a Hollywood landmark that still stands not too many miles from where he works today.

When that job ended, Hanna was once again pounding the pavement looking for any kind of employment. The Depression had spread its great gray wings over the country and there were few jobs to be found. After a long search he found a position washing cars at a service station on Sunset Boulevard. A week later, he received a call from the newly formed Harman–Ising cartoon studio, with whom he had interviewed—apparently without success—during his search. Now they were offering him a job. Gladly hanging up his soggy shoes, he accepted the offer—and found himself still in the washing business.

His new place of employment seemed straight out of a cartoon. Twenty to twenty-five people were squeezed into a tiny space above a dress shop and a garage. The studio had also appropriated one corner of the garage and fixed it up with shelves and a sink. This was Bill Hanna's workstation. Amid the mechanics and automobiles in various stages of disassembly, he washed cels.

Necessitated by the financial pressures of the Depression, this drudgery was an early form of recycling. After each cartoon had been recorded on film, the clear celluloid sheets, or "cels," on which drawings had been inked and painted, were gathered up, taken down to the garage, and cleaned so that they could be reused for the next cartoon.

After several months of enduring dishpan hands, Hanna was promoted upstairs to the realm of the ink and paint people, where he quickly became head of the department. Many workdays stretched until midnight as he enthusiastically chewed over story ideas with Rudy Ising, one of the studio's owners, a night owl whose workday began at noon.

It was at this point that Bill's years of wailing on the sax paid off. Hugh Harman, the studio's other owner, needed music and lyrics to be written for some of his cartoons, and in an opportune twist of fate, Hanna was the only one in the studio who had the musical expertise required for the job. Once again Hanna excelled at his appointed tasks, and in less than a year he went from timing frames to music to directing the animation. Soon he was also writing scripts for the cartoons.

At about this time, MGM charged executive Fred Quimby with the forbidding task of setting up and running its new in-house animation unit. Because the studio had previously contracted its cartoons out to Harman-Ising, Bill Hanna quickly came to Quimby's attention and he was soon hired.

Meanwhile, three thousand miles away, Joseph Barbera was also making his way toward MGM and, eventually, "The Flintstones."

Bill Hanna and Joe Barbera in a caricature by Tony Benedict.

JUST WHAT IS THE BASIC DIFFERENCE BETWEEN YOU AND MR. HANNA?

William Hanna, c. 1930.

On March 24, 1911, Joe Barbera was born at 10 Delancey Street on New York's Lower East Side. After four months his family moved to Brooklyn; otherwise, Barbera comments, "I would've become the head capo of something."

Barbera soon discovered he had a talent for drawing, and he entertained himself by duplicating pictures out of books. In parochial school the nuns took advantage of his talent, and kept him so busy copying religious scenes onto the blackboard that his mother objected, worried the chalk tableaux were taking precedence over his schoolwork.

Barbera continued to draw during high school, but upon graduation, with the Depression hitting full force, an artistic career seemed a remote possibility. With jobs at a premium, he was willing to take any position he could find—liking the work was no longer a requirement. "I still don't know how I arrived in a bank," he says wryly. "From day one I cannot add; I hate figures."

An early Joe Barbera cartoon that appeared in a 1931 issue of *Collier's* magazine.

Although he loathed his job at the Irving Trust Company on Wall Street, he couldn't afford to quit. Finally, with nothing to lose, he decided to try sketching his way out of the bank. Inspired by the cartoons in the *New Yorker, Saturday Evening Post,* and *Collier's,* he sat home at night, dreaming up ideas and illustrating them.

Every day at lunchtime, the minute the clock struck noon, Barbera shot out the door and uptown to submit his sketches. In a race against time, he rushed from subway station to magazine office to subway to another magazine, and then back to the bank, where a "beady-eyed" man sat and marked down the time of his return.

It was exhausting and depressing because each time he dropped off his latest creations, he picked up the previous week's submissions—rejected. Eventually one of his drawings was accepted, and at the age of eighteen, Joe was flying high. As he sold more and more drawings, his self-confidence soared. He was, however, still working for the bank.

During this period, after seeing a Disney cartoon, Barbera became fascinated with animation. He wrote to the great animator Walt Disney. "My one and only fan letter," he recalls, "and I got a letter back saying he was coming to New York and he'd call me. Fortunately, he didn't. When you went to Disney, he was the number one man and you were one of the disciples and you just vanished."

Although a job at Disney never materialized, work in animation was right around the corner. An instructor at Pratt Institute, where Barbera was taking night classes, knew of his interest in animation and arranged for an interview at the Famous studio, home to Popeye the Sailor. The meeting went well and Barbera was given a trial position.

Taking several vacation days from the bank, Barbera went to work painting in cels. After one day he was promoted to inker, where he traced the animator's pencil drawings onto the cels with india ink. On the fourth day, over lunch with another inker, he discovered the man had been at the same task for two years, and Barbera decided that banking was better

Dick Bickenbach, an animator and layout artist since the 1930s, was responsible for all the major layouts on Hanna and Barbera's Tom and Jerry cartoons at MGM. "He was instrumental in getting down a lot of the poses and animation work that enabled ['Tom and Jerry'] to get that really fluid style," explains Jordan Reicheck. "And for television, he was a key figure in putting together the whole style we know as Hanna-Barbera."

When MGM closed its animation department and Bill and Joe opened their own shop, Bickenbach was among the charter members of their new team. After helping to bring Ruff and Reddy, Huckleberry Hound, and their cronies to life, he was given the task of grooming "The Flintstones" for television success. He began by taking Ed Benedict's original models and changing them so they could be animated with less effort, "rubberizing them so they would move around easily and it wouldn't take you all day to draw the characters," he explains. "The first thing [we] did was eliminate a finger on the hand. . . . Anything you could do to cut down the costs was important," he adds, "because you had to do a lot of drawings."

FRED FLINTSTONE

Bickenbach's contributions to "The Flintstones" didn't end after his simplification of the characters. As the show's layout artist, he worked on most of the episodes for the entire six seasons. "The fun part about layout," he says, "is that you see the cartoon differently. . . . When you animate, you get a scene and you think of that scene as the [whole] cartoon; but as a layout man, you look at it as a whole production, everything going together. You enjoyed it more because you knew what the whole story was and you pre-planned it. Of course, Joe would preplan it to you. He had his own ideas and I would add. It was a cooperative deal. We had to do [the episodes] so fast we didn't have time to fight over what we had."

"Two years [of inking], I'd go nuts. That was the end of my career in animation."

—Joe Barbera

than inking. "Two years," he remembers saying to himself. "I'd go nuts. That was the end of my career in animation."

Or so he thought. The Depression continued to plague the country, and a short time later the Irving Trust Company laid off its bachelor employees, keeping only those who were married with children. Liberated from the job he hated, Joe felt as if an enormous weight had been lifted from his shoulders, and with his free time he decided to go down to Greenwich Village "and see how they starved with panache." On Broadway he bumped into a friend who sent him to the Van Beuren studio, animators of the famous feline Felix the Cat.

Barbera went, but as he tells it, "I sauntered in, no interest whatsoever." He had been in the cartoon business and he didn't like it. Nevertheless, feeling the effects of the Depression, when he was offered a job, he took it. Barbera was now an in-betweener, the person who does the drawings in between the animator's key sketches. He excelled at the job and soon came to enjoy the cartoon business. Every night he went home and practiced drawing until the early hours of the morning.

Barbera's hard work and persistence paid off. Within six months he was made an animator. He was learning fast, and soon found himself with a new employer. When the Van Beuren studio lost its contract with RKO Pictures, it was forced to close, and Barbera left Felix behind and went to work for Terrytoons in New Rochelle, New York. Here he and seven or eight coworkers were recruited by Fred Quimby for the new MGM animation department. Although most jumped at the opportunity, Barbera wasn't entirely certain he wanted to leave.

He was sitting at his desk, pondering the decision, when a hand reached over his shoulder with his paycheck. Barbera was delighted to see a ten dollar raise. Suddenly, remaining at Terrytoons seemed like a pretty good idea. "And as I'm thinking this," he says, "the hand comes over and I hear a grunt, 'Made a mistake,' and the check disappears. A few minutes later, back comes the check, and you can't believe this, they had cut the ten dollars down to five. Now, it's these little things that make you change your mind. The minute that happened, I was gone."

He moved to California and in 1937, within the halls of the MGM cartoon department, Bill Hanna and Joe Barbera met for the first time.

Bill Hanna and Joe Barbera, c. 1967. That the partners have been in business for over fifty years is to many a minor miracle. But to the two men the solution was simple. Barbera dealt with the networks, the writers, and the voice actors. "And I took it from there," says Hanna. He involved himself with the layout artists and animators, the shows' timing and music as well as orchestrating how many feet of animation footage were shot per show per week.

A year went by before they were teamed on their first joint venture, a seven-minute musical cartoon. That first piece of animation has long been forgotten, but the partnership it produced has not. It is said that Joe Barbera could sketch a storyboard faster than the drawings could be pinned up. And Bill Hanna possessed an uncanny understanding of comedy tempo. Together they honed their skills, and a year later, in 1939, they teamed up for a very special project.

They wanted to develop a cartoon series with staying power, one with characters that audiences would want to see over and over again. The result of this collaboration was "Tom and Jerry." The winner of seven Academy awards, this ever-dueling cat and mouse team kept Hanna and Barbera happily planning gags for twenty years.

Then in 1957, they abruptly found themselves, along with the rest of the MGM animation department, gainfully unemployed. With television eating away at the profits from movie ticket sales, MGM decided it made more sense to reissue already-made cartoons than to create new ones. It was the end of an era, and for many animators it was the end of a salary. Bill and Joe were in shock, as was the rest of the industry. The other studios followed suit, and soon there were no animation jobs to be found.

49

The other terrific team, Fred and Barney, bathed on TV for Softsoap in episode P–92, "The Flintstone Canaries." "Good for babies and brontosaurus' too," they sang in the tub, "use a great big hunk. Better go out and buy a bar soon, before they call you skunk."

Joe Barbera (above, left) and Bill Hanna (above, center) act out a scene from a "Tom and Jerry" cartoon for Fred Quimby, the head of MGM's animation department.

Jerry Mouse and Gene Kelly have a heart-to-heart talk (right) in a scene from the 1941 MGM classic, *Anchors Aweigh.*

Tom Cat (far right) eagerly awaits his tiny adversary's reation in the 1941 MGM cartoon, "The Night Before Christmas."

With no one offering them work, Hanna and Barbera decided to take matters into their own hands and open their own studio. And with remarkable foresight, they decided to court the entity that had cost them their jobs, television. At the time the only cartoons on TV were ancient theatrical releases, and animation made exclusively for television was unheard of. It was going to be a tough sell.

Armed with a storyboard about Ruff and Reddy, a quick-thinking cat and his dim-witted dog pal, Hanna and Barbera went in search of a distributor to market the show. Screen Gems, a subsidiary of Columbia Pictures, picked up the program and sold it to NBC, but there was a giant catch.

When Hanna and Barbera made the switch from the big screen to television, they revolutionized the way cartoons were produced. After the movie studios closed their animation departments, the fledgling Hanna-Barbera Studio was able to employ the top men in the business—and they took advantage of that opportunity. "They hired people who knew how to get the most out of the minimum of action," says Tony Benedict, a studio writer and animator during the "Flintstones" days. "They got the best writers available because everybody was out of work. Bill and Joe really saved the animation business. . . . I look upon this as a very significant achievement."

Hanna and Barbera utilized this tremendous talent pool in a whole new way. Because it was too costly to animate in the old theatrical style, with more than 25,000 drawings in one five-to-seven minute cartoon short, they pioneered techniques that allowed them to use as few as 3,500 drawings for the same length cartoon and still produce an engaging, entertaining product. Along the way those techniques became not only an art form but perhaps the most unique house style in the history of animated cartoons. Called limited animation, this style had been used before—but never with the inventiveness of Hanna-Barbera.

The Hanna-Barbera Touch

Most Hanna-Barbera characters, for example, whether man, woman, or animal, have collars on which their heads pivot; this means there are no long swan-like necks to animate. Neither are there elbows, knees, or ankles to draw, all of which saves valuable time, and therefore money. Instead, the legion of Hanna-Barbera characters—each definite individuals with their own quirks and mannerisms—were imbued with personality quotients that tipped the scales and took the audience far beyond the simple drawings.

Backgrounds—especially in the early days—were often pared to the barest essentials, sometimes resulting in what insiders refer to as "the endless living room." To avoid painting a long, detailed background behind a walking or running character, the studio would paint two small sections, or fields, that could be joined together and interminably repeated. After the character had moved from the first field to the second, the original field was placed at the end of the second, allowing the character to move back onto it. "You can keep running on that band all day and you've only painted two fields," Bill Hanna explains.

Conversation was another aspect of Hanna-Barbera's streamlined style. Moving only the characters' mouths eliminated the time consuming and therefore costly need to animate the entire figure. The delivery was enlivened by not only the skills of the voice actor but by clever plot twists and pratfalls. "Joe was the gatekeeper," Tony Benedict recalls. "He was the only one who looked at anything. If it made him laugh, he bought it and then threw in some hilarious stuff."

And therein lies the real genius of Hanna and Barbera. Not only were they able to keep the action high and the viewer immersed in the plot, but they created characters that audiences loved and with whom they could identify. It was a unique style, to be sure, but in bringing animation to television, Hanna-Barbera allowed for the creation of many now classic cartoons, including "The Flintstones."

THEN I CREATED MAGILLA GORILLA AND HEAVEN AND EARTH... AND ON THE SEVENTH DAY BILL AND I RESTED.

The Flintstones

Barney airborne on the flying machine he invented in episode P–2, "The Flintstone Flyer," the second episode produced, but the first to air on ABC (facing page).

Buoyed by the success of "Ruff and Reddy" (below), Hanna and Barbera went on to produce "Huckleberry Hound," which won an Emmy Award its first season. "He was playing on television at six-thirty or seven at night," Barbera recalls, "and in the colleges and bars they had signs: No tinkling of glasses during the screening."

Opening day at the brand-new Hanna-Barbera studio (above). From left to right, Dick Bickenbach, Howard Hanson, Joe Barbera, George Sidney, Bill Hanna, and Charlie Shows.

The budget for a five minute cartoon would be $2,800. At MGM, the budget for a cartoon of the same length had been $45,000 to $65,000.

Bill and Joe took a deep breath and agreed to the terms. If they were to make a living, they realized, it would mean doing things very differently. The creativity and innovation they mustered in order to accomplish this goal set precedents for cartoon television, and in a few short years the genre of limited animation had been created. Under Hanna and Barbera's guidance, Huckleberry Hound soon followed Ruff and Reddy, along with Yogi Bear, Quick Draw McGraw, and a galaxy of stars who are still cherished today.

And when surveys revealed that sixty percent of Huckleberry Hound's audience was over nineteen years old, John Mitchell's idea to create another animation breakthrough—the very first adult-oriented TV cartoon—seemed logical, even feasible.

If they were to make a living, they realized, it would mean doing things very differently.

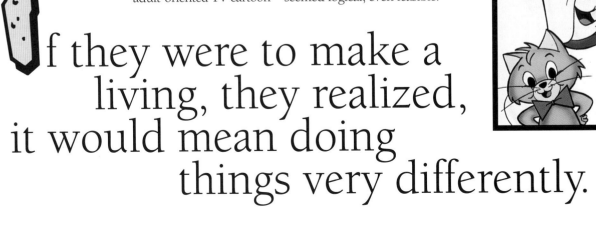

CHAPTER THREE

Animating 10,000 B.C.

From the paneless windows that make it so easy to gossip with your neighbors and eavesdrop on your wife, to scenes of Dino welcoming his master home, animating Bedrock was a challenge, a time-consuming team effort to produce some fourteen thousand individual drawings per episode. Each show utilized the skills of over two hundred artists and technicians, took about five months to complete, and required, by studio calculations, 6,300 coffee breaks. Every bit as complex as one of Fred's get-rich-quick schemes, the step-by-step creation of a "Flintstones" episode was a long and involved process. Each episode did, however, begin at the same point—with model sheets. Essentially mug shots of the cartoon world, these pages showed front, back, and side views of each character, relative height and size, and all identifying marks—in Wilma and Barney's case, whether or not their eyes have pupils. The reason for this was to

Staff members on the Hanna-Barbera production team in 1966 included: top row from left, Arthur Pierson, Neal Barbera, Steve Nakagawa; second row, Iwao Takamoto, Jerry Eisenberg, Alison Victory Leopold; third row, Don Watson, Willie Ito, Alex Lovy, Maxine Hoppe; fourth row, Barbara Krueger, Alison Victory Leopold and Jayne Barbera, Jerry Eisenberg and Iwao Takamoto, Barbara Krueger; Bottom row, Alison Victory Leopold and Jayne Barbera, Dana Chukovich, Alison Victory Leopold and Dana Chukovich (facing page).

"I doubt if a single script went through without at least five rewrites."

—Lew Marshall

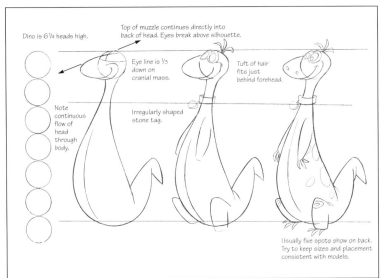

Dino is 6¼ heads high.

Top of muzzle continues directly into back of head. Eyes break above silhouette.

Eye line is ⅓ down on cranial mass.

Tuft of hair fits just behind forehead.

Note continuous flow of head through body.

Irregularly shaped stone tag.

Usually five spots show on back. Try to keep sizes and placement consistent with models.

The most recent model sheet for Dino (left). As with all the show's characters, his teeth are rarely seen. "They didn't want any teeth unless it was a tooth gag," says Dick Bickenbach, seen above at his drawing board with layout artists Willie Ito (foreground) and Jerry Eisenberg. "They didn't really look good."

maintain consistency; every animator working on every episode must always draw the characters in exactly the same way. What would Wilma— and the viewing audience— think if Fred went to work tall and portly and came home fifty pounds lighter and four inches shorter? To this end, the model sheets also served as a fashion guide for each character, illustrating everything from the color of Fred's quirky tie and the number of spots on his suit to the shape of Wilma's rocky pearls, so reminiscent of June Cleaver's. During the course of the series, the studio artists also produced model sheets for the Modern Stone Age wacky inventions, and before long their efforts resulted in a catalogue that was over an inch and a half thick.

Armed with this background material, the storyboard artist went to work. Drawing in comic strip style, a quick sketch was created for each scene, and dialogue and sound effects were written under each panel.

Meanwhile, as the storyboards were being drawn, the show's voice actors were busy in the recording studio, taping their lines for the episode. Under the guidance of a voice director, "Flintstones" actors were often required to play many roles, changing age, nationality, social status, and even species several times per show.

After the dialogue was recorded and edited, a track reader—an individual with endless patience and precision—measured the time it took to speak each word in the entire episode and recorded his figures on exposure sheets. Using these sheets,

Joe Barbera (left) and Daws Butler review a storyboard.

Dot eyes. It's a peculiar physical trait that only Wilma and Barney seem to share on "The Flintstones." They have neither pupils nor irises nor eyelashes, merely coal black orbs with which to express emotion and view the world. Possibly this glazed look is from years of dealing with Fred; after all, they are the two who bear the brunt of his personality most frequently.

"I don't think there was really any intellectual reason for it," Iwao Takamoto, a key creative employee of Hanna-Barbera throughout its history, explains, "except probably the fact that they wanted to establish a different look on each character. . . . I think there was a period when the use of dot eyes was a way of getting something a little out of the ordinary."

They've Got the Look (Sort of)

While shaping the characters' personalities, this stylistic technique also presented problems for the animators. "You couldn't get that sidelong glance as easily as with what are usually used as eyes," Takamoto says. "Some of the animators used to cheat in sort of a lash line so they could move the eye back and forth, but usually it wasn't quite strong enough to really 'read' in completely. Body language then becomes very important. I use the angles of the head, cocking the head and eyebrows. If you look at someone straight on, you can stare at them, but if you do this (he cocks his head), it becomes a stronger look."

Actually, Barney is lucky to have even dot eyes. Originally he had what Takamoto refers to as "Little Orphan Annie eyes," two round circles that weren't even filled in. When asked why this was altered, he speculates that the Rubble orbs were changed in production for the sake of expediency. It was easier to color the entire eye black than to paint an interior. "It doesn't make any difference," he adds, "except to people who like to look for things like that."

One of the other early details that has since been refined is the hair of Barney's wife, Betty. In the first episodes of the show she used to have blue lines—comb marks—that added detail to her hair. But with the advent of the photocopier, the pencil drawings, instead of being hand inked, were Xeroxed onto the cels, and all linear work became uniformly black. So Betty's hair has no lines, but it doesn't have any gray either. Maybe it's because she's one of those lucky people who stays youthful for years—or perhaps it's because she's not married to Fred.

WILMA

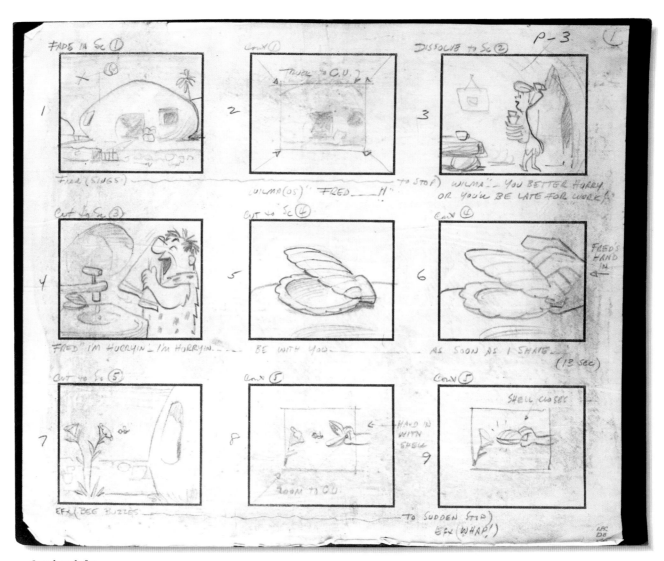

Storyboards for episode P-3, "The Prowler." Animators used these sketches—drawn nine to a page—along with model sheets as guides to create the actual cartoon (above and facing page).

Joe Barbera (seated) reviews a storyboard with writer Tony Benedict.

the animators determined how many frames, or individual drawings, were necessary to form each word on a character's lips. When Fred bellows "Wiiiillmaaa!" his mouth and facial movement must match the shout exactly, his mouth closing just as the yell ends.

The director also used the exposure sheets—and the storyboard—to time the action. Everything, from how fast Dino runs across the room to how long Fred stares dumbfounded at his wife, was precisely paced. "It's like directing actors," Bill Hanna explains. "How long or how fast a character should walk or how mad he gets, it all has to be determined. You're editing, timing, and giving directions to the animators all at the same time."

At this stage in production, layout artists, working from the storyboard and script, drew pencil backgrounds with character posings indicated in each scene. When the layout work was complete, the animators—who draw the characters and make them move—and the background painters took over. In animation, each sequential drawing is only marginally different from the next, but when viewed in rapid succession—on consecutive

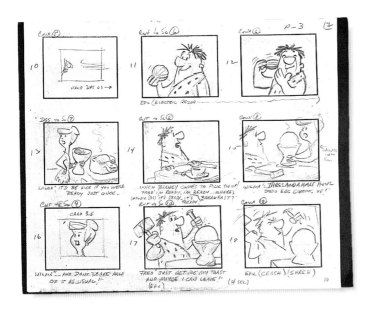
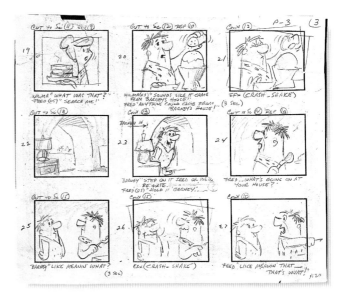
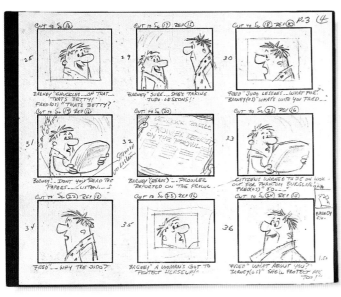
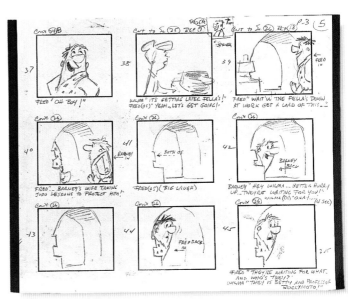
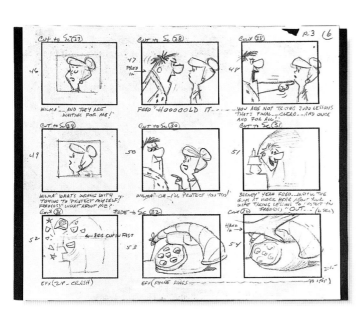
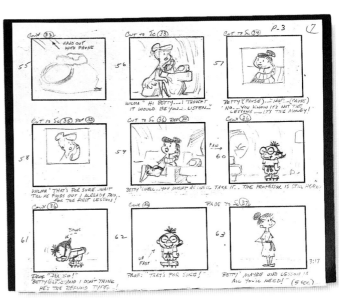

The Hanna-Barbera staff were multi-talented, many being animators as well as writers, layout artists, and designers. "They had this great crew," Tony Benedict says, "people who could do all these things that now take dozens of people."

Clockwise from above: associate producer and layout artist Alex Lovy; layout artist Don Jurwich; animator Gerry Hathcock at his drawing table; Frank Pakier, head of the camera department; "Flintstones" comics and Little Golden Book illustrator Harvey Eisenberg; animation checker Midge Sturgis; layout artists Willie Ito, Jerry Eisenberg, and Dick Bickenbach; Fernando "Monte" Montealegre, head of the background painting department.

The Flintstones voice actors at a recording session (facing page). From left to right, Alan Reed as Fred, Jean Vander Pyl as Wilma, Bea Benaderet as Betty, and Mel Blanc as Barney. Joe Barbera directed the sessions. "He used to say, 'This is a cartoon!'" Vander Pyl recalls. "'It's gotta cut! Gotta be sharp!' ...you can't just talk like you would in an ordinary show. It doesn't come over in a cartoon."

Half the fun of "The Flintstones" lies in the convoluted storylines that ensure that nothing in Bedrock is ever quite as simple as it should be. An evening of dining and dancing degenerates into a mad chase, peaceful vacations become wild, and even a trip to the doctor's office is fraught with misunderstandings. But despite the fact that most of these occurrences are in some way linked to Fred, it's not his fault—it's that of the writers'. And they were a special breed. A cartoon storyteller must be able to think in very visual terms, and in fact, many "Flintstones" writers bypassed the scripting process entirely and went straight to the storyboard.

In "the old days," Bill Hanna explains, "It was not uncommon to have a writer draw rough sketches of his story." Warren Foster, for example, wrote and storyboarded all but nine of the first year's episodes. "For years," Joe Barbera says, "we didn't have writers per se; we had people who would draw the story, the same way I do. That was a great way of saving time. For instance, Mike Maltese and I would settle on an idea. Mike would start drawing the story as he moved along, and he'd be laughing his head off. Then he'd show me the pages and say, 'Here, look at this,' and I'd see it and we'd both be shrieking. . . . He got the attitude and that's what's important."

But not everyone appreciated the Hanna-Barbera brand of humor as animator and story director Lew Marshall can attest. As Hanna-Barbera's liaison to the ABC network, his job was to submit the studio's storyboards to the network and help smooth out any problems that might arise. "It was horrible," Marshall recalls. "The network had complete approval on scripts all the way through. I doubt if a single script went through without at least five rewrites."

The network's chief concern was with prehistoric parodies, like the Polarock camera, that might result in litigation, as well as with matters of a puritanical nature. While Wilma was

"expecting," they banned the use of the word *pregnant*, and showing the visual likeness of anything resembling a stone toilet was absolutely forbidden. Nevertheless, Fred and Wilma made sitcom history as the first prime-time couple to share a double bed, previously a prohibited activity of the highest order. Marshall, however, doesn't recall the event as any type of milestone. "I guess it just happened," he says matter-of-factly.

Examples of layouts. Blue pencil sketches (above) indicate the positions of the characters in a scene from episode P-13, "The Girls' Night Out," while a blue line shows where Wilma will be positioned in a kitchen scene (below).

"Bill and Joe really saved the animation business."

—Tony Benedict

frames of film—the characters come to life. A good animator must possess a comprehensive understanding of movement—both human as well as dinosaur—and the ability to breathe life, personality, and emotion into his subjects. One look at Fred's grouchy countenance is enough to demonstrate that the "Flintstones" animators were experts.

When the animation drawings were complete, they were transferred to clear celluloid sheets called "cels." The cels were then hand-colored—on the back so as not to overpaint the black outlines—using preassigned color schemes. After painting, the cels were checked for consistency, and cel wipers gave each one a final cleaning to remove any dust or debris.

Now it was lights, camera, and action! Sort of.

Unlike a motion picture camera, an animation camera is stationary, exposing only one frame of film at a time. To keep the elements in precise alignment, special pegs are used to hold each cel in place and prevent it from shifting. A painted background was laid down first, then one or more character cels were put on top of it. In a scene where Dino licked his beloved master's face, for example, Fred's body might be on one cel, Dino's tongue on another, and Fred's hands pushing him away on a third, all laid over a background of the

FLINTSTONES,
　　meet the Flintstones,
　　They're a **MODERN** Stone Age family.

　　　From the
　　town of **BEDROCK**,
　　　They're a page
　　　　right of history.

　　Let's ride
　　with the family down the street,
　　Through the **COURTESY**
　　　of Fred's two feet.

When you're with the Flintstones,
Have a **YABBA-DABBA-DOO** time,
　　A dabba doo time,
　　We'll have a gay old time!

Everybody knows the theme song to "The Flintstones." Boisterous as Fred himself, it bounces out of the screen and sweeps the viewer into Bedrock and the story. But when the show first ran in 1960, Fred did not slide off his dino-crane and race home to take his waiting family to the drive-in. It wasn't until two years later that the familiar song and visuals debuted.

In the original opening of each episode, "Rise and Shine," a booming instrumental, backed the credits while Fred drove home from work, twisting and turning around the bends of Bedrock. With a jarring halt, Fred parked in his garage and went into the house to watch television. And while the familiar closing credits depict the family at a drive-in restauraunt and then returning to put the cat out for the night, in the original closing Fred turned off his television and went into the bedroom to cover the bird cage before putting Baby Puss out the front door.

Hoyt Curtin, the musical director for the studio, composed the classic piece that accompanies the present opening. But, according to Curtin, "putting your finger on the right music was tough. After all, you have to figure out—What kind of music does a caveman play? Anything dated, we felt,

would detract from the visual feeling of the caveman period. We had to pick instruments that would give a sound illusion of bigness, of dinosaurs and prehistoric giants."

Although the piece they finally decided on perfectly sets the tone for the entire series, it started out as just a bit of background music. "The very first show has Fred and Barney digging a swimming pool together," Curtin explains. "Of course, they get into an argument. And subsequently they feel guilty about fighting with each other. So under this action I had to come up with a sad musical accompaniment. And when I jazzed it up, this slow, sad music actually became 'The Flintstones' theme." With the music written, Bill Hanna's lyrics were added, the tune was recorded with five singers and a twenty-two-man jazz band, and the rest is musical history.

Flintstones' living room. A glass plate secured the cels, the cameraman triggered his shutter, and a single exposure was shot, creating one cartoon frame. The cels were then changed and the next frame photographed. On average it took eight hours to film one minute of animation as it would appear on TV.

After the film was developed, a work print was made. The print was matched to the voice track by the film editor, who, along with the director, reviewed the episode for any errors that needed to be corrected. Once any required revisions were completed, sound effects were chosen from an entire library of bonks and thuds, and then the music was selected. Finally, all of the audio and visual elements were combined to produce a final print for broadcast.

Although it took months to produce the twenty-four minutes of animation that comprised a single "Flintstones" episode, the work has paid off for the show's creators. For today, Bedrock is being viewed by new generations of fans, and it is just as alive now as when the shows were new.

Clockwise from above: writer Alan Dinehart; writer Dalton "Sandy" Sandifer, layout artist Alex Lovy, and writer Tony Benedict; layout artist and designer Iwao Takamoto and layout artist Jerry Eisenberg; animator Irv Spence; voice actor Janet Waldo; writers Mike Maltese and Warren Foster.

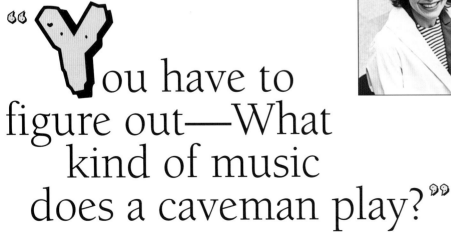

"You have to figure out—What kind of music does a caveman play?"

—Hoyt Curtin

One of the giddier aspects of life in Bedrock is the abundance of inconsistencies. From architecture to car design, few things ever appear quite the same way twice. The Flintstones' house, for example, seems to sport a different front door in every episode. That important portal through which Fred slams his way each evening when he arrives home from work is red one week, blue the next, and white the week after that. Sometimes a chimney graces the exterior; just as often, it doesn't exist. Occasionally the home sits on a corner or across from an empty lot; in other episodes the topography of the surrounding neighborhood is entirely different.

When Fred takes that first step into the living room after work each night, the avid "Flintstones" watcher knows the decor will have changed. Sofas and chairs change color and style with each episode, and incidental items such as pianos and bookcases appear and disappear from week to week as the storyline dictates.

Out on the street, there's the matter of cars, which transmogrify faster than the furniture. One minute Fred's vehicle is a sporty two-seater coupe; in the next scene it's a four-

seater Flintmobile that conveniently enables the Flintstones and Rubbles to go out on the town together. The observant "Flintstones" fan will also note that the steering wheel switches from the left to the right side of the car with no warning. And whenever anyone enters or exits the car, the soundtrack provides the satisfying thunk of a slammed door. This seems normal enough—until you realize Flintmobiles have no doors.

To the die-hard "Flintstones" fan, these idiosyncratic inconsistencies are characteristic of the show's more endearing qualities—quirkiness, erraticism, and just plain fun. And inanimate objects are not the only evolving items in the "Flintstones" world. Over the years Fred's employer has had his name (and occasionally his looks) changed from Mr. Boulder to J. J. Granite to Joe Rockhead to, finally, Mr. Slate.

While Fred and Barney usually belong to the Royal Order of Water Buffalos, their great fraternal organization is often referred to as the Loyal Order of Water Buffalos (and was originally called the Loyal Order of Dinosaurs, back when the series began).

Trying to keep track of it all is enough to keep a Flintstonephile busy for days. "There were inconsistencies in the writing and in the animating," admits Dick Bickenbach, "because the main emphasis was getting the show on the air. . . . Different [animation] units did the show differently, even drew the characters differently."

"Different storyboard men or layout men would be assigned to a given episode," Iwao Takamoto explains. "Many times a lot of the specifics would be bent or adjusted to accommodate the story to make it more effective. Many times there was a good reason for it. Other times it was an arbitrary decision. It just sounded better."

CHAPTER FOUR:

Neolithic Profiles

As any die-hard "Flintstones" fan will tell you, Fred, Wilma, Barney, and Betty are not just cartoon characters; they're people. Okay, so they have only eight fingers and six toes each, they wear the same animal skins almost every day, and they (the men, at least) can survive falling off buildings, being hit by boulders, and motoring miles underwater without serious damage. But they're still people—Stone Age people—living in a society that reflects the post-war optimism that existed at the time the cartoon was created as well as the eon in which they live.   Bare feet are acceptable even in the finest restaurants, although one would never presume to enter an establishment such as the Chateau Rockinbleu without first donning a tux. Women are expected to heft steaks bigger than themselves and still display dainty figures. It is socially correct to eat your own weight in food at one sitting, and while knocking someone flat with a stone newspaper is not considered polite behavior, neither is it malicious.   Some Neolithic mores bear a striking resemblance to those of the late fifties, when the show was first conceptualized. Wilma and Betty do not work outside the home, and should the thought flit across their minds, they are careful to get their husband's approval first. Fred and Barney refer to them as "the girls," a phrase that would make a woman fume today. (Equitably, however, Wilma and Betty do speak of their husbands as "the boys.") Women are never seen in slacks (but for that matter, neither are the men), and except in cases of dire emergency, such as when Fred believes Wilma to be pregnant, the boys never stoop to do housework or even prepare a meal. (Barbecuing is different.) Although these customs are indicative of a patriarchal society, the women are the ones who actually rule the homes—at least in Fred and Barney's case—and they certainly are the ones who get to spend the money.

Despite, or perhaps because of, these prehistoric standards, the residents of Bedrock present an endless source of fascination to modern man. Recently excavated, the following biographical material helps to illuminate the real lives of, if not the rich, certainly the famous Flintstones and their friends.

MINIMUM OF BODY BEND·

FRED FLINTSTONE
FRACTIOUS, INFECTIOUS AND FUN

Wild-mannered Fred Flintstone, dino operator by day, devoted hubby by night, is a man of many facets. He appears to be a simple blue-tie worker, but a wealth of other personae also lie buried beneath his big belly. He's been a beverage formulator—inventing soft drinks with disastrous results—as well as a carnival operator, restaurateur, and private investigator, to name only a few of his temporary careers. Not one to pass up the opportunity for easy money, Fred has never let incompetence stand in his way.

A big bear of a man with an expressive face that can turn from jovial to grouchy and back again in an instant, Fred is instantly recognized by the black-spotted, orange tunic he favors as daily wear and the severe cowlick that gives him a perpetual "bad hair" day. He describes his eyes as "robin's egg blue," although they appear black; his hair is raven; and despite a daily shave with a bee-powered razor, his cheeks sport the stubbled look later adopted by the men of "Miami Vice."

Along with his childhood pal, Barney Rubble, Fred attended Bedrock high school and served a stint in the Army. After marrying Wilma Slaghoople, he began a career as a dino (dinosaur) operator at the Bedrock Gravel and Quarry Company (also known as Slate Rock and Gravel, and sixteen other variations). Although he has an excellent working

Fred in a scene from a viewmaster reel.

Fred in an early Ed Benedict sketch (facing page).

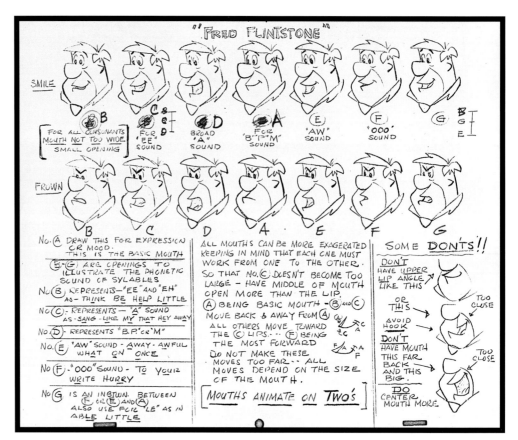

An early guide to animating Fred, drawn by Ed Benedict (right).

"Fred is part Archie Bunker, part [Jackie] Gleason," says Iwao Takamoto. "He is hard-headed until he realizes he's done something wrong or hurt someone, and then he is devastated," (facing page).

relationship with the dinosaurs, his dealings with his boss, Mr. Slate, are fraught with tension. This could be because Fred has no compunctions about playing hooky from work—any reason will do; it doesn't have to be a good one.

At home, Fred and Wilma epitomize the lifestyle of the Modern Stone Age family. Occasionally Fred and Barney slip out for a meeting of the Royal Order of Water Buffalos—a men's-only haven of boisterous guys in silly hats—or for an evening of pin tumbling down at the bowling alley. But Fred is just as happy at home with his wife and daughter, Pebbles, to whom he reveals endless patience and a surprisingly gentle nature. With adults, however, Fred has little tolerance, a trait that bothers everyone but him. But when you're a big, burly guy like Flintstone, you have to throw your weight around—there's not a whole lot else you can do with it.

Not one to pass up the opportunity for easy money, Fred has never let incompetence stand in his way.

ALAN REED
THE "ORIGINAL" FRED

Bellowing at Wilma, belly laughing with Barney, cooing at Pebbles, or bombastically introducing himself to television producers, whatever Fred Flintstone does, his big, booming voice makes it more entertaining. That voice was provided by Alan Reed, a native New Yorker with whom he shared another trait—his weight.

A versatile performer in stage, film, and television, it was in radio that Reed made his mark. He began his broadcast career in 1926, and during radio's Golden Age he played in thirty-five shows a week. If he had ever contracted laryngitis, the entire radio network would have had to shut down—or scramble for a dozen other voices.

As an actor on Broadway, Reed starred in "The Pirate," appeared with Fredrick March in "Hope for a Harvest," and played Falstaff in Shakespeare's "The Merry Wives of Windsor." Moving to Hollywood, he began acting in movies—in roles as diverse as Pancho Villa in *Viva Zapata* and Sally Tomato in *Breakfast at Tiffany's*.

Although always an actor, Reed—like Fred Flintstone—often found other ways to supplement his income. Early in his show-biz career, he and a partner opened a candy business, specializing in pecan pralines. The pralines sold well during cool weather, but when the summer heat set in, the confections turned to what Reed described as "an interesting gray color, like secondhand oatmeal." He also polished brass on transatlantic liners, stocked packing crates in a cotton goods house, worked as a gym instructor, a real-estate salesman, and a newsreel commentator, not necessarily in that order. In 1954, Reed opened an advertising-novelties and business-gifts showroom, a business that he continued to run during his tenure as the Modern Stone Age family man.

On television, he played in many of TV's acclaimed "theaters": Four Star Theater, Lux Theater and many other monochromatic playhouses. But his most famous television role, of course, was the one in which he was never seen, Fred Flintstone.

"Reed would carry on," Joe Barbera recalls of the big actor. "He'd be loud and noisy and shift around . . . but the timbre of his voice was the important thing. Reed had warmth."

"Dad was universally loved," says his son, Alan Reed, Jr., "and I can say that from a distance, believe it or not. . . . There was something about him that I know was a big part of the Flintstone character. I know it was in his voice."

"He melted when it came to children," adds Reed's wife, Finette. "With kids he would stand on his head. He was really a big kid at heart."

When he died in 1977 at the age of sixty-nine, Reed left fifty-six years of big-hearted, big-voiced entertainment behind him, and as Fred Flintstone, a legacy of laughter for generations to come.

The Flintstones

Fred Flintstone and Alan Reed, the man who provided his voice (facing page). "The secret is," Joe Barbera explains of the process of evaluating voice actors, "if you can close your eyes and smile to yourself, you know there's humor in the voice. If it makes you laugh, then you're halfway home."

Always the master of the situation—at least in his own mind—Fred is very vocal about his thoughts and feelings, thanks to the voice of Alan Reed. Reed's voice was so distinct that, unlike his costars, he rarely played incidental characters on the show. "Alan got his nose out of joint because they would never let him do the extra parts," recalls Jean Vander Pyl. "He really sounded too much like Fred. Once in a while they'd let him do a truck driver or something, but mostly he just did Fred because his voice print came through."

HENRY CORDEN
ROCK-SOLID
REPLACEMENT

When Alan Reed passed away, he left a very large pair of bare footprints to fill. Fortunately for Bedrock and television viewers everywhere, Henry Corden was available. Corden, who had provided the voice for many incidental characters on the show as well as Fred's singing voice in the 1966 theatrical release, *The Man Called Flintstone*, recalls having a strange mixture of emotions at the time. "Of course I felt sorry about what had happened to Alan. But then, honestly, I was also excited about the opportunity to do the voice of Fred."

Although he was a respected actor in his own right, having appeared in dozens of movies and TV shows, Corden was very jittery about slipping into Fred Flintstone's skins. "On the

Fred works with several dino-cranes—Mildred, Lulu Belle, Rocky, and Hugo—all of whom share a common foible: dropping boulders on Mr. Slate. Despite this shortcoming on the part of his equipment, Fred is a superior workman; his boss has discovered on more than one occasion that the company can't be run without him.

first day of recording I was downright shaky and nervous. I had to go in with all of these people who had been on 'The Flintstones' since the beginning, and here I was succeeding the lead role . . . and what happened was, I got so nervous that my nose began to bleed! I felt so embarrassed. I thought, 'These people are going to think I'm not a pro.' That's how intimidated I was about the whole thing. Once we got past it, it was fine."

A seasoned veteran of stage, screen, and television, Corden lists innumerable film credits, which run the gamut from Cecil B. DeMille's *The Ten Commandments* to slapstick vehicles with Abbot and Costello.

Corden knew Alan Reed prior to becoming involved in the series—or at least he was fairly intimate with Reed's act. "I started out doing stand-up comedy," he says. "And one of the first things I did as a teenager . . . was stolen directly from a one-reel comedy Alan had been in, in which he did Shylock in various dialects. . . . I did his whole routine in my act. Years later I told him about it. But isn't it odd that I'm now doing the voice of a character Alan created, and so many years ago I started out doing Alan."

In fact, Corden originally performed his interpretation of Fred Flintstone as a direct impersonation of Alan Reed, but gradually, he eased more and more of his own voice into the character. "What Alan was doing was Alan. He didn't have to alter his voice, really," Corden explains. "When I first started doing Fred, I was doing Alan. Now I do it a little more like Gleason, who the character was patterned after in the first place."

Since assuming the role of Fred, Corden has provided his voice for over a dozen different "Flintstones" series and specials, continuing to allow Fred's joyful "Yabba-Dabba-Doo!" to ring out over the Bedrock countryside.

"**F**red is part Archie Bunker, part [Jackie] Gleason."

—Iwao Takamoto

**WILMA
FLINTSTONE
THE WOMAN
BEHIND
THE MAN**

Although Wilma Flintstone worked as a waitress before her marriage, and was briefly the hostess of an early evening television show, "The Happy Housewife," she is known chiefly as the better, more sensible half of Fred Flintstone (someone has to be) and the mother of Pebbles. Generally Wilma is a steadying force, providing a balance for Fred's impulsiveness. And while some would call her sly guidance manipulative, she prefers to think of it as "husband management."

A model housewife, Wilma even dusts Fred's bowling ball on a regular basis (she discovered that it's Fred's favorite place to hide his extra cash). Although she's usually thrifty, Wilma does have a weakness for shopping sprees and wishes that she didn't have to return things after "taking them home on approval." The original mall maniac, she often disappears into the heart of the Macyrock Department store, wielding a credit card and yelling, "Chaarge—it!"

Wilma has learned to live with Fred's frequent money-making schemes, which generally blow up in his face. And although she would never dream of wearing the pants in the family (they haven't been invented yet), she's always there to set things straight after disaster strikes.

Wilma brings Fred his lunch in a scene from episode P–1, "The Swimming Pool."

While some would call her sly guidance manipulative, Wilma prefers to think of it as "husband management."

JEAN VANDER PYL
THE WILMA WITHIN

Where would Fred Flintstone be without Wilma, the only person who can keep him in line? And where would sensible, and sometimes sardonic, Wilma be without Jean Vander Pyl? A native of Philadelphia, Vander Pyl has provided the Bedrock native's voice since the earliest promotional tape was made of "The Flagstones." But unlike Wilma, Vander Pyl was not your average housewife, Stone Age or otherwise. With an acting career that spans more than a half century, she can lay claim to cartoon vocals of almost every variety, as well as radio, television, and stage performances.

The love of acting hit Vander Pyl when she was fourteen years old, and only three years later she was discovered by a radio producer who was impressed by her multiple-voice talents. In addition to garnering a long list of radio credits, Vander Pyl has also appeared on television in everything from dramas to commercials. Once she arrived at Hanna-Barbera, she provided almost too many voices to count. "In the first few seasons of 'The Flintstones,'" she says, "Bea Benaderet and I did almost every female character in the script."

One character that occupies a special place in her heart is that of baby Pebbles. When it came time to cast the voice of the baby Flintstone, Vander Pyl recalls, she was ready. "Joe Barbera said, 'Okay, who wants to do Pebbles?' and I immediately spoke up. I'm usually not that bold, but I wanted to do Pebbles. I wanted just the right voice for that cute face." In fact, Jean was so closely tied to her roles of Wilma and Pebbles that her son Roger was born the same day that the "Blessed Event"—Pebbles's birth—aired on national television.

"I was pregnant that summer that we were recording, but the cast didn't know it," she says. "Only Bea knew it because we were such close friends. One day I wore a dress that made me show more in the tummy, and Joe Barbera looked at me and said, 'Jean . . . that dress on you, it makes you look pregnant.' I looked at Bea and she looked at me and I said, 'Well, I am.'

"Their faces all dropped," after which there were congratulations, hugs, and some razzing. "Joe said, 'Well, you didn't have to go that far, Jean. I know you want realism, but c'mon, this is ridiculous.'"

Having rehearsed her "watery gurgle" for days in advance, Vander Pyl was right on cue with Pebbles' first sounds, "Abba gabba goo!" "That was a special show for Alan and me," she says. "When Pebbles was born, I had a lump in my throat and I looked at Alan and we both welled up with tears, especially when Alan, the new daddy, called her 'Pebbly-Poo.' It was very tender. We loved it because we almost never got the chance, ever, to have tender moments as Fred and Wilma."

"I wanted her voice to command enough authority to run the house, but retain an equal amount of warmth."

—Jean Vander Pyl

Jean Vander Pyl purposely patterned her voice after Alice Kramden of "The Honeymooners." "That's why I made Wilma sound sort of flat and nasal," she explains. "I wanted her voice to command enough authority to run the house, but retain an equal amount of warmth."

BARNEY RUBBLE
BEST BUDDY
ON THE BLOCK

Fred and Barney jam with Hoagy Carmichael in a scene from episode P–31, "The Hit Song Writers."

With his infectious chuckle, sunny outlook on life, and ability to overlook the grumpiest disposition (i.e., that of longtime pal Fred Flintstone), Barney Rubble is Bedrock's quintessential good neighbor. Born in Graniteville, Barney grew up in Bedrock alongside Fred. The two attended Bedrock High together, met their wives together, and mutually spend a great deal of time evading their wives' ire—in short, sharing all the ups and downs of Modern Stone Age male bonding. Most people find Fred to be overbearing and difficult, but Barney doesn't let these flaws stand in the way of true friendship.

Initially wary of Fred's enthusiastic and impulsive schemes, Barney usually ends up throwing caution to the wind and enjoying himself, even though, when the plans backfire—and they always do—he is the one blamed for their failure. The important thing in Barney's mind is to be a loyal buddy, and this he performs flawlessly. Left to his own devices, he would be just as happy staying at home and spending the evening with his lovely wife, Betty, and their super-strong son, Bamm-Bamm.

The great mystery that continues to puzzle Flintstonephiles is the burning question of what Barney does for a living. Like that of Ozzie Nelson, Barney's career has long been a matter of speculation. Leaving the house every weekday morning with Fred, he appears to head for a regular nine-to-five job. But what he does every morning after Fred drops him off at the corner is anyone's guess. He's been seen entering the offices of Pebbles Co. Rock and Gravel, as well as those of Slate Rock and Gravel. He has worked temporarily as a furniture repossessor, a travel agent, and has joined Fred in an entrepreneurial stint as co-owner of a drive-in restaurant. These are all matters of public record. But why does he never stay at one job? And why is his position so rarely referred to? His wife, Betty, once let slip to an acquaintance that he is in "top secret work."

In a scene from show P–17, "The Hypnotist," Barney hangs out with some new friends.

MEL BLANC
OL' BUDDY BARNEY

Great actors often have to be coerced into accepting great roles. Initially Clark Gable adamantly refused to play Rhett Butler in *Gone with the Wind,* and when Mel Blanc was offered the role of Barney Rubble, he flatly turned it down. As he explained in his autobiography, *That's Not All, Folks!,* Joe Barbera called and asked if he'd be interested in playing Fred's good-natured neighbor, a "prehistoric Art Carney."

Blanc thought the show sounded like fun, but with more than four hundred voices of his own under his belt, he was not interested in imitating another actor. Barbera countered with the proposal that he didn't have to impersonate Carney.

"'Tell me,'" Blanc recalled him asking, "'how do you think Barney Rubble would talk?'

"'Well, I dink he'd talk like dis, Joe, with a silly hiccup of a laugh.' And I broke into, 'A-hee-hee, a-hee-hee-hee.'"

Barbera gave him the part and Mel Blanc became Barney Rubble. In fact, he performed Barney so uniquely that most people never realize the voice of Barney was also the voice of Bugs Bunny, Daffy Duck, and a legion of other Warner Bros. cartoon characters.

Stepping forward several years in time and then back to the Stone Age, Blanc became not only the voice of Barney Rubble, Fred Flintstone's best buddy, but also of Fred's pet dinosaur, Dino. Then, in January of 1961, Blanc's cartoon career almost ended entirely when his Aston-Martin was hit head-on by a college student who was racing his father's Oldsmobile on Sunset Boulevard. Lying comatose for three weeks, encased in plaster casts, Mel returned to consciousness only when his doctor began to ask questions not of him but of Bugs Bunny. Waking up, he responded with a weak, "I'm okay, Doc."

Except for a handful of episodes that were voiced by Daws Butler (of Yogi Bear and Huckleberry Hound fame) during the worst of his incapacitation, Blanc recorded every one of the 166 episodes of "The Flintstones," including more than forty that were done while he was flat on his back, recovering in the bedroom of his Pacific Palisades home, with a microphone suspended above him and the rest of the cast gathered around the bed. After the series ended, Blanc continued to record countless specials, television commercials, as well as the 1966 movie *The Man Called Flintstone,* until his death in 1989.

Lying comatose for three weeks ... Mel returned to consciousness only when his doctor began to ask questions not of him but of Bugs Bunny.

FRANK WELKER
NEW BUDDY BARNEY

"Barney is just a loyal friend. No matter what Fred does, he's always forgiving and always there for him. I think in life that's nice, that you have that one friend you can always count on." So says Frank Welker, who has voiced Barney Rubble—and Dino—since Mel Blanc's death.

Welker actually began doing Dino while Blanc was still with "The Flintstones." "I was at a recording session, voicing various incidental characters, when they wanted (Blanc) to do Dino, Welker recalls. "Because it was painful for him, they asked me if I'd like to give it a try, and I did. Then Mel had me do Dino the last few sessions because it was very hard on him. [After Blanc's death] when the auditions went out for Barney, I was one of the guys who tested. Being in love with the character for so long, it was just a real treat to get the part."

Matching his own voice to Blanc's Barney was more a matter of "working with Mel and being a fan," than of being given specific instruction, Welker says. "It's trying to produce as closely as possible what he was doing. Obviously you're not going to get it exact, but you try to get as close as you can."

Welker had been a Hanna-Barbera voice actor long before winning the roles of Barney and Dino. In fact, the first animation project he did was "Scooby Doo, Where Are You?" in which

In an outtake from episode P–2, "The Flintstone Flyer," Barney displays his operatic talent.

he played Freddy. Cast in the role because of his youth, Welker learned his technique at the Hanna-Barbera studio, much of which he credits to Joe Barbera. "Joe really taught me how to read animation and also gave me a lot of opportunities. . . . He would say, 'I got a dinosaur here. Anybody wanna try it?' John Stephenson would do it and then Don Messick would do it and then Henry Corden, and then I'd raise my hand. 'You wanna try it? All right, Welker, you do it.'" And Welker demonstrates a very convincing dinosaur growl.

"That was one of the really neat things about animation in the old days," Welker recalls fondly, "the way Joe would cast the incidental parts. Everybody had an opportunity to show off, have a great time, and show latitude in their range . . . and it was really in this way that Joe introduced me to doing all these various voices."

"Barney has a mind of his own," says Iwao Takamoto, "a certain perspective as far as values are concerned. . . . He doesn't have quite the flamboyance Fred has. He's sort of laid-back and sort of cool."

BETTY RUBBLE
COMRADE IN ARMS

A slim brunette with a lively sense of humor and a ready giggle, Betty likes to rhapsodize over film hunks like Stony Curtis, but the real love of her life is her husband, Barney. They met shortly after high school, and his Mel Tormé magnetism and rakish Neolithic looks soon swept her off her feet. For his part, Barney was entranced by Betty's breezy girl-next-door charm, and before long Betty Jean McBricker became Mrs. Barney Rubble.

Betty and her new husband stepped easily into suburban life in Bedrock, making a cozy home out of their cave on Cobblestone Lane. Clever as well as considerate, she lets Barney believe he's the head of the house while she manages everything—including Barney himself—from behind the scenes.

When Fred steps over the line and insults Barney once too often, it is Betty who encourages him to stick up for himself. Barney may not be proud, but his wife is. She is also a terrific mother and manages her son and his pet, Hoppy the hopparoo, as easily as she does Barney, enjoying every moment she spends with her family and friends.

With Wilma living right next door, Betty never lacks for activity. Sharing magazine hubby quizzes, trips to the beauty shop, and even camping expeditions with her comrade in arms, her days are full.

BEA BENADERET

Betty Rubble is the quintessential next-door neighbor, fun, perky, but definitely the costar where script action is concerned. Bea Benaderet, the first voice of Betty, seemed to specialize in just such roles. From "Ozzie and Harriet" to "Petticoat Junction," Bea's characters were always secondary ones. "She was a pro when we brought her on board the show," Joe Barbera recalls of Bea, "but because of the character and the casting, Betty played a number two banana in the women's part of it. I guess we never gave her any leads and wrote a story that she took over, which I think was a mistake; we should have." Close friends in real life with Jean Vander Pyl—just as Betty and Wilma are close—Benaderet left the show in 1964 and passed away in 1969, having left as a legacy four seasons of giggly Betty episodes. She may not have been the top banana, but she was a cheerful neighbor, and what sitcom, Stone Age or otherwise, could do without one?

GERRY JOHNSON

Around the time that Bea Benaderet left Bedrock in 1964, Joe Barbera was a guest on "Panorama Pacific," a television show hosted by Gerry Johnson. While Barbera was there, he sketched some silly characters and Johnson supplied the appropriate voices. Delighted with her skills, Barbera offered her the role of Mrs. Rubble, a position that she accepted and held until the original series ended in 1966.

GAYE AUTTERSON

Although original "Flintstones" episodes were no longer being made, Betty still lived next door, as evidenced by the Saturday morning "Pebbles and Bamm-Bamm Show." This time she was voiced by Gaye Autterson, a seasoned stage actress who had decided to exploit her natural ability for mimicry and sent Hanna-Barbera a demo tape featuring her renditions of Pearl Bailey and Mae West. Thanks to the tape, she was cast as several female basketball players in a cartoon show about the Harlem Globetrotters, and when the need arose she segued into Betty Rubble number three.

B. J. WARD

The latest Betty, B. J. Ward, has definitely passed the tests for inclusion into the exclusive Betty Rubble Voice Club. After all, she has successfully auditioned three times. "I remember auditioning for the part years ago," B. J. explains. "At the time they weren't doing a lot of 'Flintstones,' and after I got the part we only did one or two shows. Later, the studio decided to do a new series called 'The Flintstone Kids' with all the characters as children. They held big open auditions and told us we had to read again." And, as if these auditions weren't enough, the same thing happened a third time. Today, in addition to providing the voice of Betty in ongoing specials of "The Flintstones," Ward—a professional singer who performs everything from country to opera—also welcomes visitors to Disney World and Epcot Center in Florida via a variety of recorded messages.

"We don't really learn much about Betty," says B. J. Ward, "because she goes along with Wilma, doesn't really strike out on her own or do anything daring. She's just a good ol' buddy to Wilma, like Ethel Mertz was to Lucy."

Bea Benaderet feigns jealousy as Jean Vander Pyl favors Barney with a kiss (top, left).

PEBBLES
FLINTSTONE
Daddy's
Dearest

At precisely eight o'clock on the evening of February 22, 10,000 B.C., Pebbles arrived at the Bedrock Rockapedic Hospital, born to parents Fred and Wilma Flintstone of Cobblestone Lane. With her turned-up nose, big, wonder-filled eyes, and sweet smile, it's no surprise that she charms everyone she comes in contact with. Her father gave her the nickname of Pebbly-Poo the moment he laid eyes on her, and he has been under her spell ever since, along with Wilma, Barney, Betty, and even Arnold, the newsboy.

The joy of Pebbles's life, other than Mom, Dad, and, of course, Dino, is her next-door neighbor and best friend, Bamm-Bamm Rubble. Banging on musical instruments in the family den or playing in the backyard, Pebbles and Bamm-Bamm make a special team, and one gets the feeling that one day Fred might actually have to think about walking down the aisle at their wedding.

BAMM-BAMM RUBBLE
THE BOY WHO
NAMED HIMSELF

Most parents must baby their babies, but in Bamm-Bamm Rubble's case it sometimes seems as if it's the other way around. His superhuman strength comes in handy around the house, whether it's moving furniture or lifting the car so Dad can change a tire. And how many parents can claim that their baby bounces them?

Bamm-Bamm is the pride and joy of his parents, Barney and Betty, who remember vividly the day they found him on their doorstep. Wielding a little club, the towheaded tyke looked up at them and exclaimed, "Bamm! Bamm! Bamm!" The Rubbles were captivated, and taking the child into their hearts and home, they immediately began adoption proceedings, and have never regretted it.

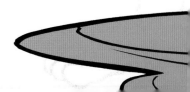

Talking with Don Messick, you would never guess that he is the childlike voice of little Bamm-Bamm Rubble. Speaking as himself, he has a deep and powerful boom that would be more at home in the chest of a news anchorman than in a towheaded tot. When told he doesn't sound like Bamm-Bamm, Messick replies, "I hope not. Except when necessary." Playing Bamm-Bamm, with his one-word vocabulary, was never boring, Messick says, because, "first of all, it was a paying job. Second, the dialogue was simple. I could have memorized it. It was fun."

Messick was hired as one of Hanna-Barbera's first voice men in the late fifties, shortly after the company was formed. Over the years he has given voice to such popular cartoon incarnations as Yogi's little buddy, Boo-Boo; Scooby-Doo; the Jetsons' semi-talking dog, Astro; and Papa Smurf. Additionally Messick voiced many incidental roles on "The Flintstones," including cops, announcers, butlers, phonograph birds, dinosaurs, turtles, skunks, and Hoppy, to name just a few. Playing several roles at once was not difficult, he explains, as long as colored highlighting pens were available to mark the different parts. "As my eye jumped from color to color, the voice changed automatically."

Of Bamm-Bamm Rubble, Arnold the newsboy, and his other "Flintstones" roles, Messick says, "Sessions were always fun. There was always a lot of horsing around with the script." But at the same time Messick notes, "Joe Barbera was very demanding. He was excellent. . . . He knew what he wanted and he wouldn't let up on us until he got it."

"Joe Barbera was very demanding. He knew what he wanted and he wouldn't let up on us until he got it."

—Don Messick

Part of the fun of watching "The Flintstones" is the element of star gazing—watching for the guest celebrities who showed up on a regularly irregular basis. One never knows when a Hollyrock hunk like James Darrock will appear, or when an episode might feature a TV host like Rocky Genial of "Peek-a-Boo Camera," who is—not coincidentally—a ringer for Alan Funt of "Candid Camera."

When Stony Curtis showed up in Bedrock, viewers were as thrilled as Wilma. Real-life celebrity Tony Curtis, who voiced the Stone Age star, remembers when he was first asked to be a guest on the show: "Someone from New York called me and said, 'Hey, listen, there's a chance they want you for this cartoon.' I thought it sounded wonderful. The next thing I knew, I reported to this recording studio. It was fabulous. I met Mel Blanc and Alan [Reed] . . . and it was thrilling to finally see who they were."

Hooray for Hollyrock

Drawn with de rigeur bare feet and a casually V-necked animal skin, Stony fit right in on Cobblestone Lane. The animators had originally attired him in an ascot tie, but hoping for a look as unabashedly Neolithic as Fred and Barney's, Curtis asked that it be erased. After all, when in Bedrock, do as the natives do. Curtis, who donated his fee for the episode to a summer camp fund, recalls the role fondly. "It was very hip," he says. "I loved doing that show."

Singer-actress Ann-Margret was transformed, via the Hanna-Barbera animation department, into singing sensation Ann-Margrock. "When they told me about it," she recalls, "I thought the idea of Ann-Margrock was so adorable and cute. Then they showed me a drawing of the character . . . and most of her was made up of bright red, fluffy hair. . . . I got a big kick out of it."

The story line has "Annie" helping Fred and Barney rehearse an act for the opening show of Bedrock's new amphitheater, but the biggest impression she made was with the song she sang to baby Pebbles. "What we wanted her to do was sing a lullaby," Barbera says. (*continued on next page*)

Hoagy Carmichael (top) goes before the mike to voice his animated alter ego. Dino (center) shows off his talents for a producer in a scene from episode P–62, "Dino Goes Hollyrock." Fred and Barney (bottom) sing with Ann-Margrock in episode P–103, "Ann-Margrock Presents."

(*continued from previous page*) "It was an original song that we composed at the studio. She was absolutely delightful, and it came out as a charming, wonderful show."

"What's interesting," the actress says, "is that all these years later . . . these little kids ask me if I'm Ann-Margrock. And now their parents come up to me also and say they first saw me on 'The Flintstones.' I'm amazed."

Songwriter and band leader Hoagy Carmichael appeared as himself in "The Hit Song Writers," the episode which opened the second season of "The Flintstones." "That was a great experience," Carmichael said of his Stone Age gig. "Guesting on 'The Flintstones' and being a part of the spoofing of the music business was fun. Although I'm seen as an animated character, the part actually makes me feel more human than anything I've ever done."

Other entertainment luminaries who appeared in Bedrock were James Darren, Jimmy O'Neill (host of the dance show "Shindig," or "Shinrock-a-Go-Go" as it was known in the Stone Age), Elizabeth Montgomery and Dick York of "Bewitched" fame, and even "smarter than the average bear," Yogi and his little pal, Boo-Boo.

Besides these illustrious few, "The Flintstones" hosted a galaxy of other stars, but they were all strictly celluloid—Stone Age impersonators of mid-twentieth-century celebrities. And because most of then were modeled on 1960s hipsters, it's now only the die-hard TV addict who can recognize Peter Gunn in Perry Gunite or Captain Amos Burke in millionaire detective Aaron Boulder.

Compared to most Stone Age families, the Flintstones and the Rubbles seem to enounter an inordinate number of celebrities. They have been rescued from rustlers by the Cartrocks of the Rockarosa Ranch, confronted in court by legendary lawyer Perry Masonry, and befriended by movie star Rock Quarry. One could spend days speculating on causes for this phenomenon, but perhaps Tony Curtis put it best when he said, "It does your ego good to wind up in the cartoons." Is more of a reason needed?

Celebrity guests of "The Flintstones" included, (clockwise from top, left) Perry Masonry, Samantha and Darrin Stephens, Ed Sullystone, Alvin Brickrock, Jimmy O'Neillstone, Ed Sullystone, Hoagy Carmichael, the Cartrocks, and (center) Ann-Margrock and Stony Curtis.

Fred consults with detective Perry Gunite in episode P–21, "Love Letters on the Rocks" (left). Samantha Stephens—played by Elizabeth Montgomery — appeared in episode P–148, "Samantha" (center). (The opening for the perky sorceress' own show, "Bewitched," was also animated by Hanna-Barbera.) Stony Curtis autographs a photo for Wilma in episode P–144, "The Return of Stony Curtis" (right).

MR. SLATE
A BOSS WITH AN ATTITUDE

Master of his own company, possessor of a classic type-A personality, a window office, and a snazzy set of spectacles, the only thing Mr. Slate does not admit to owning is a first name. He does have one—allegedly Sam, although he also answers to George—but he prefers to go by the more dignified "Mister." Slate believes that a person carries more clout without the excess baggage of a friendly first name. After all, with a personable moniker like George, it might be difficult to supervise with authority.

And it's tough to be a gravel quarry executive, particularly when you have employees like Fred Flintstone. Mr. Slate works long, hard hours sequestered inside his plush office, and it's difficult to glance outside the window at Flintstone and know he's poised and ready to dash home the second the five o'clock whistle blows—especially when he's always calling in sick anyway.

The astute observer may have noticed that Mr. Slate's appearance changed drastically at one point. Originally he was short, round, and pudgy, not at all the executive type. But after extensive cel-ular surgery he reemerged, taller, slimmer, balder—much more the corporate tycoon about town.

Tycoon or not, Slate is completely dominated by his wife (she doesn't appear to have a first name either, except for "dear"), and perhaps this is why he yells so much. She frequently interrupts his work to dictate grocery lists or insist that he sell charity ball tickets, as well as perform other forms of labor not at all befitting a busy executive.

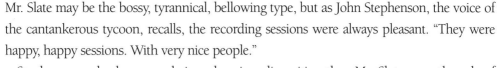

Mr. Slate may be the bossy, tyrannical, bellowing type, but as John Stephenson, the voice of the cantankerous tycoon, recalls, the recording sessions were always pleasant. "They were happy, happy sessions. With very nice people."

Stephenson, who has more hair and a nicer disposition than Mr. Slate, won the role of Fred's dictatorial employer after auditioning for "The Flagstones." Although he had more than a decade of radio experience, it was to be his first-ever animation performance. "At the time, you see, we didn't realize it was going to be such a big thing. It was just a job," he admits. "But right from the start I loved cartoon work."

It was while working on "The Flintstones" and other Hanna-Barbera shows that Stephenson realized he had a knack for celebrity impersonations. "Joe Barbera would call me in the evening before a taping, just out of the blue, and ask me if I could do Howard McNear, or Frank Nelson, or W. C. Fields, or whatever. And I would literally try it out over the phone for him. And often he'd say, yes, that'll be fine. The next day I'd be doing that voice for a cartoon."

Stephenson felt that there was a special quality about "The Flintstones." "There really was an ensemble feeling about the cast since we all knew each other from radio. But it was more than that. We knew how to create images in the mind simply through the voice. To us, 'The Flintstones' was like a radio show that they took and animated."

A spike-nosed exile from the planet Zetox, the Great Gazoo is one of Bedrock's least recognized citizens, invisible to all but children, animals, and the "two prehistoric dum-dums" he is forced to serve— Fred Flintstone and Barney Rubble. Says Harvey Korman, who voiced Gazoo, "I'm surprised they went with me. When you look at the little tyke, you'd expect he'd have some other kind of a voice . . . not this cultivated sort of English butler's voice."

Like all loyal family pets, Dino does a lot more around the house than exercise his owner. He barks at strangers, babysits Pebbles, slurps down Shlump and Dino-Gro (his favorite foods), and watches TV. A sensitive creature who adores his family, especially Fred, he has been known to run away from home when his feelings are hurt.

She loves her daughter, Wilma, is scornful of her son-in-law, Fred, and when visiting the Flintstone household, she attempts to rule it with an iron fist. Her name is Mrs. Slaghoople, and if you're Fred Flintstone, the best way to get along with her is to get out of her way.

With a scratchy pre-adolescent voice and orange hair, Arnold the paperboy sounds like Walter Denton and looks like a prehistoric relative of Howdy Doody. He is, in reality, a lad with a strong pitching arm and a quick mind, and nearly every time he throws the paper, it flattens Fred.

CHAPTER FIVE

Back by Popular Demand

On April 1, 1966, the last original episode of "The Flintstones" was broadcast. Although the show was still popular, Joe Barbera says plainly and simply that, "The sponsors wanted something different. . . . The advertising agency invited us to a dinner and we all had a big table with toasting and drinking, and the next day they dropped us." Apparently they felt they could get more for their money with something fresh and new, even though only six years earlier, "The Flintstones" was so unique that sponsors were afraid of it.   Audiences, however, were not as fickle. Instead of quietly fading away, those six years of Stone Age television—166 episodes—quickly began airing as reruns, becoming classics in their own right and forming the foundation for a veritable plethora of television specials, Saturday morning spin-offs, and even two big-screen movies. Today, Hanna-Barbera proudly proclaims, "every hour of every day someone somewhere

A posterior view of Fred drawn by Ed Benedict (facing page).

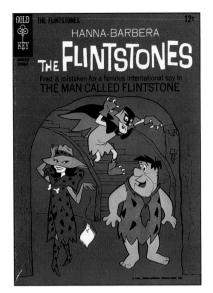

The comic book version of the 1966, motion picture *The Man Called Flintstone*. On the cover (above), Fred's attention is snared by Tanya, a sultry agent of the evil spy master, The Green Goose.

The title treatment for "The Flintstones Comedy Show," NBC's strongest performer in its Saturday morning line-up during the 1980–81 season (below).

in the world is watching 'The Flintstones.'" This is heady stuff for any series, much less one that almost didn't get sold and later was unceremoniously dropped.

Less than a year after the series ended, the Flintstones were back in a project that was even more ambitious than weekly television: the 1966 animated motion picture, *The Man Called Flintstone*. Taking its cue from the barrage of suave-and-sophisticated James Bond stories that were currently thrilling audiences, the animated film detailed the adventures of Fred Flintstone as he conquered the forces of evil while standing in for his look-alike, secret agent Rock Slag. Seven musical numbers enlivened the action, including the title song—a take-off of the James Bond hit, "Goldfinger"—and a romantic ballad, "Pensate Amore," sung by Louis Prima. Boasting more than a half million cels in the finished production, the show was a success, with critics employing phrases such as "entirely charming" and "considerable ingenuity in development."

With the success of the movie, things seemed to quiet down in Bedrock, and for the next several years the Flintstones stayed out of the public eye except for television commercials produced by Kraft General Foods—the makers of Pebbles cereals—and Miles Laboratories, creators of the Flintstones Vitamins. Then, in 1971, Hanna-Barbera decided their Stone Age offspring had been on hiatus long enough, and put them back to work in a new Saturday morning series, "Pebbles and Bamm-Bamm." Bypassing several important growth stages, Bedrock's favorite tots were now teenagers attending Bedrock High where, not surprisingly, they became embroiled in a variety of misadventures along with their pals Moonrock, Penny, and Wiggy. Pebbles was voiced first by Sally Struthers—soon to gain fame as Gloria of "All In the Family"—and then by Mickey Stevens and Russi Taylor, while the vocals for Bamm-Bamm were provided by Jay North, previously known to audiences as Dennis the Menace.

When "The Flintstones Comedy Hour" made its Saturday morning debut in 1972, the original episodes of "Pebbles and Bamm-Bamm" were combined with newly written ones, vignettes, gags, and a dance of the week—including the always popular Pterodactyl Flap. The new stories endowed Bamm-Bamm with a cave buggy, a morose jinx of a buddy named Schleprock (voiced by Don Messick), and a quartet of cycle-riding arch nemeses, The Bronto Bunch. Ever recyclable, these episodes were rerun in the 1973–74 season under the banner "The Flintstones Show," aired as "Pebbles and Bamm-Bamm" through the fall of 1976, and then were syndicated as segments of "Fred Flintstone and Friends."

Returning to the prime-time limelight for the 1977–78 season, Fred and his

pals headlined in two NBC specials, "A Flintstone Christmas," in which Fred fills in for Santa on Christmas Eve, and "The Flintstones' Little Big League," where Fred and Barney get into trouble coaching Pebbles and Bamm-Bamm—suddenly regressed to preteen years—who are playing on rival teams.

In 1979, Fred and company could again be seen on Saturday mornings. "The New Fred and Barney Show" took thirteen original "Flintstones" episodes and redubbed Henry Corden's voice over that of Alan Reed, and Gay Autterson's over Bea Benaderet's. Things got more exciting with "Fred and Barney Meet the Thing," in which "Flintstones" episodes were paired with tales of a teenage protagonist who with his Thing Ring could turn himself into a superhero. As if all this was not enough, "The Flintstones Meet Rockula and Frankenstone," a 1979 prime-time special, detailed the adventures of the Flintstones and Rubbles on vacation in Rocksylvania.

Then things really got complicated. Several months later, viewers could watch the Flintstones for an hour-and-a-half each Saturday morning when "Fred and Barney Meet the Shmoo"—the Shmoo being a friendly shape-shifter whose normal appearance was a sort of ghost-in-a-sheet blob—was added to the line-up. The next year, 1980–81, the ninety-minute "Flintstone Comedy Show" premiered, featuring six segments: "Flintstone Family Adventures," "Pebbles, Dino and Bamm-Bamm," "Captain Caveman" (the Superman-type alter ego of Chester, copyboy for the Bedrock Daily News), "Bedrock Cops" (would you believe Fred and Barney?), "Dino and Cavemouse," and "The Frankenstones." The 1980–81 season brought more prime-time specials as well: "Fred's

A presentation board for "Pebbles and Bamm-Bamm" that was used to sell the show to the networks (above). Pebbles and Bamm-Bamm as young adults (below).

"As we moved through time, we always tried to come up with something else that could be done with 'The Flintstones.'"

—Joe Barbera

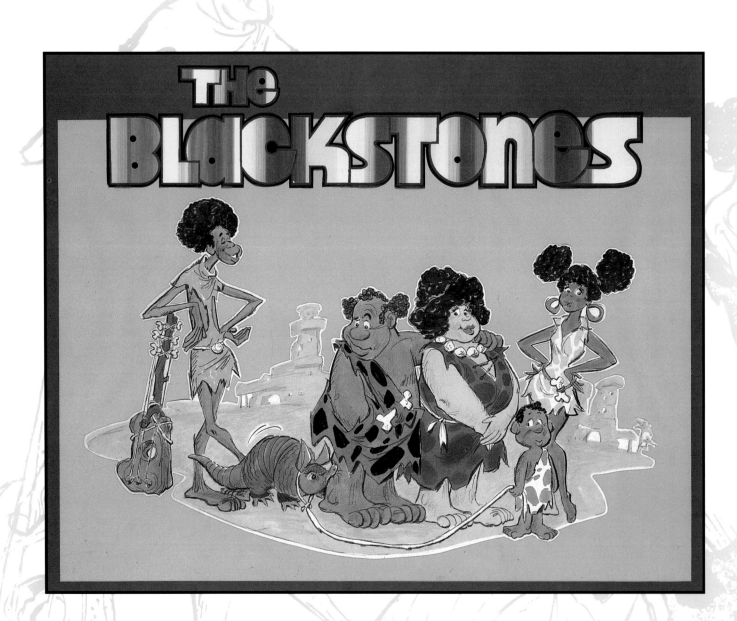

The Blackstones

An unusual item that was recently unearthed from the Hanna-Barbera archives is a piece of artwork labeled "The Blackstones." "It was a short-lived development," Iwao Takamoto recalls. "We were going to do a black Flintstones. If you think back to 1976, it was a pretty fresh idea. We had a lot of different ideas, that they would be neighbors of Fred and Wilma, for example, and there were many twists and turns you could take on something like a black family living next door that would have provided us with lots of different stories. I suppose Fred could have been nervous about someone different living next door. He could have taken an Archie Bunker attitude, and then ended up accepting them totally.

"I did the artwork," Takamoto says. "Model sheets were never done because it was just something Joe was talking to the networks about, saying we had a couple of ideas, just to get a reaction from them. If they responded strongly, then it would have been worthwhile for us to make an effort."

"I thought when I got the idea," Joe Barbera relates, "they were going to jump on it with open arms, but I was a little ahead of myself. Nobody bit on it, which I think was a big mistake. In fact, what I'm trying to do now is revive it."

Final Fling," in which Fred mistakenly believes he has only twenty-four hours to live; "The Flintstones' New Neighbors" (those lovable Frankenstones); "Wind-Up Wilma," detailing the distaff side of pro baseball; and "Jogging Fever," which tracked Fred's trials and tribulations as he trained for the Rockston Marathon.

In this presentation board for "The Flintstones' Little Big League," Pebbles and Bamm-Bamm are much younger than the preteens who appeared in the actual program (above).

Iwao Takamoto feels that one of the things that kept "The Flintstones" popular through the years was the sense of something softer beneath all of the slams and bangs. "A certain gentleness existed," Takamoto explains. "There was always that nice family kind of attitude, an underlying set of morals."

"Fred is obviously a loving man," echoes Henry Corden. "He's up front with everything; he has the sweetness and the ability to say, 'Hey, I'm sorry, I goofed.' "

For whatever reason, "The Flintstones" continued, returning to the airwaves year after year. But trying to think of new directions was sometimes a challenge. "As we moved through time," Joe Barbera says, "we always tried to come up with something else that could be done with 'The Flintstones.' Every year we were trying to go out there and sell something. In 1985," Barbera recalls, "I had lined up a presentation for what was then a very hot item called the Cabbage Patch Kids. They were moon-faced dolls, pretty ugly, but they were the big rage. Everybody had one."

At the time Squire Rushnell was the head of children's programming at ABC, and Joe had already sold him on the show. Now Rushnell had the task of selling the idea to both the creator of the Cabbage Patch Kids and the distributors, who had the license to sell them.

"Well," Barbera says, "when Squire went and pitched the idea to them, they weren't talking to each other and each refused to agree to a deal if the other was involved. So there I was sitting in New York, and Squire Rushnell is on the phone pleading with these people to go ahead on the deal, and them rejecting every move he made. Finally he threw down his hands, hung up the phone, and said, 'I can't do this show.'

"At that moment, a spark struck, and I said, 'Why don't we do "The Flintstone Kids?" We

The Flintstones Kids were junior versions of their adult selves, right down to the clothing. B. J. Ward, the most recent Betty, provided the voice of young Betty Jean, while Henry Cordon—the voice of Fred after 1977—played the voice not of young Freddy, but of his parents, Ed and Edna.

How does one modernize a Stone Age city, yet still retain a Cenozoic feel? This was the task facing Iwao Takamoto in 1991 when he began production of the Flintstones' most recent adventures, "I Yabba Dabba Do!" and "Hollyrock-A-Bye Baby."

In the two made-for-television movies, the Flintstones and Rubble families have grown with the times. Wilma and Betty now run a catering business and Pebbles and Bamm-Bamm are young adults with careers of their own. So it was only logical that the town of Bedrock grow as well. "We wanted a world that looked like our world," says Bill Hanna. "In the original "Flintstones," low flat buildings filled the city and suburbs. Now high-rise buildings and apartments need to exist next to the family neighborhoods. Part of the fun of "The Flintstones" is its parallel of our world."

Thoroughly Modern Bedrock

To achieve this goal, Takamoto asked for a reassessment of Bedrock. In the early days the architecture had a primitive feel with rounded buildings that resembled hollowed-out boulders with slabs of granite for roofs. But over the years, Takamoto says, "spotty material was churned out." The artists in charge of backgrounds "were very qualified except that they couldn't understand the Flintstones and they made square buildings."

Takamoto's modernization plans resulted in what was almost a contradiction in terms—newfangled high rises with a Stone Age twist. As a finishing touch, Bedrock was further enhanced by a citywide painting program. "In updating the backgrounds," Takamoto explains "I had the artists pay particular attention to the play of light and shadow on the buildings. The result is a more artistic, painterly feel." Aided by a new, brighter palate of colors and Takamoto's strict attention to detail, Bedrock has moved into the Neolithic nineties, with all of the conveniences and nuisances of "modern" life.

In 1994, with the release of a live-action motion picture—which immediately became the highest-grossing Memorial Day weekend opening in movie history—the Flintstones added a new item to their already impressive roster of credits. Simply yet eloquently titled *The Flintstones,* the movie authentically duplicates the feel and texture of the show's original episodes. "We did our best to re-create the signature moments," says Brian Levant, the film's director, "but we go beyond that."

Flintstones - The Movie

"It's all here," producer Bruce Cohen agrees. "We took the basics—the two families, the kids, Dino, and what would be a typical Flintstone plot—then we embellished. "Fred and Wilma," he explains, "represent sort of the traditional American couple who believe in family, who believe in raising a child, and who want to better themselves so they can make a nicer life for themselves, their friends, and their children. We took that as our background and created from it our conflict—which is that Fred is lured by the trappings of success."

John Goodman, cast in the role of Fred, won the part without an audition; in fact, without even knowing he was being considered. In 1989, while Steven Spielberg, executive producer of the live action version of *The Flintstones,* was directing Goodman in the film *Always,* he was struck by the resemblance between Goodman and Fred. "Steven asked me, no, he

actually told me, that I was going to play Fred Flintstone for him," Goodman recalls. "I just kind of sat there and smiled."

Elizabeth Perkins plays Wilma to Goodman's Fred, the Rubbles are fleshed out by Rick Moranis and Rosie O'Donnell, and, in a casting coup, Elizabeth Taylor, who hasn't been seen on the big screen in fourteen years, steps into the meaty role of Wilma's mother, Mrs. Slaghoople.

For the perfect prehistoric setting, the film makers chose Vasquez Rocks in the Santa Clarita Valley as the location for Bedrock. "It's this terrifically stark, exciting visual landscape that just naturally lends itself to become Fred's street," explains Bill Sandell, production designer for the film.

From RocDonalds Restaurant with it's arched golden tusks to the Toy-S-Aurus store, the sets are authentically Flintstone—cock-eyed, giddy—and gently poke fun at contemporary society. And as all those who've seen the film agree, it is undeniably boisterous, bright, and big. As Brian Levant explains, "We needed to bring Fred Flintstone to life and feel the full range of emotions with him, so that at the end of the movie you haven't had a snack . . . you've had a full meal."

just have them all young, Fred and Barney and Betty and Wilma as little kids. We even take Dino and make him a puppy.' He bit on it immediately and that was the birth of 'The Flintstone Kids,' all due to the fact that we couldn't sell the Cabbage Patch Kids."

In the show, which ran from 1986 through 1988, the Flintstones were ten-year-olds, living in Bedrock with their

"Steven [Spielberg] asked me, no, he actually told me, that I was going to play Fred Flintstone for him."

—John Goodman

friends and parents, a device which provided a delightful opportunity to peek into their roots. The show revealed that in the Flintstone home, Edna, Fred's mother, was the undisputed boss, with husband Ed—the owner of Flintstone's Fix-It service—and son Freddy cringing at the sound of her voice and the taste of her cooking. Barney's parents, Flo and Robert Rubble, lived next door, where Flo painted canvases while "Honest" Bob—Freddy's idol—ran a car dealership. Wilma's father, Sidney Slaghoople, operated a computer service (his PCs—prehistoric calculators—consisted of a monkey with an abacus in the back of the monitor); her mother, Doris, was active in the PPTA (Prehistoric Parents and Teachers Association). Betty's parents, Mel and Janet, ran Bricker's Quick Stop, a Neolithic convenience store.

The friends included poor-little-rich-girl Dreamchip Gemstone, junior private eye Philo Quartz, and bespectacled Nate Slate, who was destined to become Freddy's boss. There was also a villain in the person of neighborhood bully Rocky Ratrock. With this cast, the show aimed to educate as well as entertain. As the "bible" for the series explains, "segments should feature stories that are full of fun, adventure, heart, and (of course) plenty of prehistoric gadgets."

The effort succeeded, winning a Humanitas Prize in the Children's Animated Category, for "its charming and witty treatment of the power of perseverance; for its touching probe of a child's struggle to grow and affirm himself; and for its affirmation that kindness and support from those around him are essential to this process." A 1988 special, "Flintstone Kids: Just Say No," addressing the issue of drug abuse, also garnered awards and acclaim—additional confirmation of the show's ability to educate imaginatively.

In 1987, Hanna-Barbera took "The Flintstones" in still another direction—the future. In the made-for-television movie, *The Jetsons Meet the Flintstones*, the first family of the Stone Age travel to the future while the Jetsons experience prehistoric life.

A scene from "Captain Caveman." When not playing the role of prehistoric super hero, the Captain's alter-ego, Chester the copy boy, worked at the Bedrock Daily News along with reporters Betty and Wilma.

"The Flintstones" in the future may, at first glance, seem a strange concept, but actually they've always kept up remarkably well with the era in which they aired. When the original series debuted, the Polarock camera was technology; now Fred and Wilma have a VCR. (Whether or not they can program it is another question.) The Modern Stone Age couple drives a motor home; Bamm-Bamm has his own computer—which prints out stone pages—and Pebbles is a woman of the Nineties with a career as vice president of an advertising agency (pretty radical when one considers that her mother could not get a job as a secretary without first asking Fred's permission).

In 1993 two television movies brought viewers up-to-date with the latest milestones in the Flintstones' lives. In "I Yabba Dabba Do!", Pebbles and Bamm-Bamm get married—as everyone always knew they would—but not before enduring all the antics and confusion that seem to accompany every Flintstones affair. Special guests of the bride and groom include an animated Bill Hanna and Joe Barbera who say benevolently of the happy couple, "They were made for each other."

Just nine months later, in "Hollyrock-A-Bye Baby," Pebs and Bammer, as they affectionately call each other, are living in Hollyrock, expecting a baby, and suffering through a visit from their parents. At the conclusion of the movie—which includes a mad chase through Hollyrock involving a motor home, a tour bus full of sightseers, a purloined bicycle, and an irate painter on foot—Pebbles finally makes it to the hospital and gives birth to twins, towheaded Roxy, who inherits her father's strength, and redheaded Chip.

Finally, in December 1993, the half-hour special "A Flintstone Family Christmas," found the older generation Flintstones and Rubbles involved with Stony, "a caveless kid from the wrong side of the tar pits," while awaiting the arrival of the newest members of the clan who were snowed in at O'Harestone Airport.

For those who grew up with the original Flintstones, seeing Pebbles and Bamm-Bamm with children of their own is somewhat unsettling. We expect them to still be infants themselves. But in Bedrock, as in the rest of the world, life goes on. Soon no doubt, Chip and Roxy will have shows of their own. After all, they're Flintstones. And even though they no longer air every Friday night, the phenomenon continues.

Scenes from "I Yabba-Dabba-Doo!" in which Pebbles and Bamm-Bamm, now adults, get married. Attending the ceremony are an animated Bill Hanna and Joe Barbera (bottom).

Two of Hanna-Barbera's favorite families finally meet in a scene from the made-for-TV-movie, *The Jetsons Meet the Flintstones* (facing page).

CHAPTER SIX: # The Bedrock Phenomenon

Since the series began, the Flintstones have been great advertising spokespeople. Within the storylines of the show, Fred promoted the Fat-Off reducing method, Wilma sang the praises of Rockenshpeel Fine Foods, and even Betty plugged Softy Skin Lotion ("the lotion that makes your skin so soft it's almost mushy")—all Modern Stone Age products that could never be found in the twentieth-century world. But the Flintstones didn't only hawk imaginary goods. They also advertised real products that any viewer could—and the sponsors hoped, would—go out and buy. In fact, during the show's first two years, the opening and closing for each episode included a friendly word from Fred, spoken on behalf of the sponsor. The program began with a sequence resembling the opening montage of the latter day prime-time animated series "The Simpsons," in which Fred zipped through town in his Flintmobile on his way home. Literally slamming into his garage, he rushed into the house,

Flintstones money, issued c. 1962 by the Whitman Publishing Company (facing page).

In 1962 Welch's began sponsoring "The Flintstones," a development that led to the conspicuous consumption of grape juice during several episodes of this time period (left).

The cardboard Wilma spraying Fred with Bactine antiseptic was used as an in-store stand-up display (right).

switched on the television, and sat down to watch—himself. For there he was, on the screen of his own TV, opening his medicine cabinet to reveal a box of Alka-Seltzer and a bottle of One-A-Day vitamins, both products of Miles Laboratories, one of the show's two sponsors.

Later, when the show broke for a commercial, the Flintstones would often be there as well, pitching still more products. In one Winston cigarette spot, Fred and Barney are standing outside while Wilma mows the lawn and Betty beats a rug. Finding it painful to view this constructive activity, Barney comments, "I hate to see them work so hard." "Yeah, me too," Fred agrees. "Let's go around back where we can't see 'em."

Retiring to the rear of the house, the boys light up a couple of smokes and spend a few moments discussing the merits of the brand. Fred then sings the Winston theme song—leaving little doubt as to why Alan Reed's singing voice was usually dubbed by Henry Corden—and just as he finishes, Wilma and Betty round the corner, ending the boys' cigarette break and the commercial.

"The Flintstones" was an advertiser's dream come true.

The storyboards illustrate a commercial for Winston cigarettes that was aired during the opening of the show.

Fred lights up for Winston cigarettes.

THE FAR SIDE
By GARY LARSON

© Chronicle Features. 1980

FRED AND WILMA

7-29

BIZARRO
By DAN PIRARO

I CALL IT 'SATIRE'

PIRARO ©CHRONICLE FEATURES 1988

The Flintstones have appeared everywhere from newspaper comics to television to toy store shelves. Joe Piscopo and Danny de Vito suit up as Fred and Barney in a scene from the 1984 HBO "Joe Piscopo Show" (top, left). A Marx Toys miniature Bedrock with plastic caves, Flintmobiles and figurines—perfect for staging one's own episodes (bottom, right).

THE QUIGMANS

7-1

"Why do we look like this? Simple. We worship Pebbles Flintstone."

From the earliest days of the show, the Flintstones have appeared in an astonishing variety of places. In the sixties, the Modern Stone Age family showed up on the menus of Pan Am Airways, allowing travelers to eat Bedrock style as they winged their way to Hawaii. Bedecked in a lei and palm frond hat, Fred presented his "favorite foods," including cream of ichthyosaurus soup, broiled triceratops tails, and plesiosaurus pudding.

And now, almost thirty years later, the Flintstones still are known to make occasional appearances on one's menu, offering new varieties of "prehistoric" food. During a Denny's restaurant promotion in 1991, a Bedrock-minded tot could choose from a selection of Stone Age treats such as tyrannosaurus waffles, prehistoric pancakes, or for lunch, a corn dogosaurus. Also available were take-home treasures such as collector plates, reusable place mats, and that standby of die-hard dino operators, the Flintstones lunch box.

For the ardent fan who wishes to meet Fred in person but is unable to make the arduous journey to Bedrock, there is no need to despair. An avid traveler himself, Fred has spent considerable time touring shopping malls and amusement parks around the world, from Universal

Studios in Florida and California, to that down-under theme park, Wonderland, in Australia. He frequently appears in parades, sometimes driving his Flintmobile, sometimes bobbing aloft as a mammoth balloon. And closer to earth, Fred-worshippers have caught the big man at Pasadena's famous Rose Bowl parade as early as 1961 and as late as 1994. His family rides with him in these events, both to temper his tendency toward hamminess and to share in the fun of hobnobbing with the fans. Fred even demonstrated a more sedate side in 1990, when he appeared at the ribbon-cutting ceremony at the National Religious Broadcasters media expo.

The Flintstones can also be seen at video stores, in books, comics, and of course, on television. It's been said that wherever you go, there you are, but it's also true that wherever you go, you're liable to run into the Bedrock bunch.

A purple-footed Pebbles, a pool inner-tube with Fred's head, and a punching bag Fred were just some of the inflatable items that were available to the avid "Flintstones" fan. For the intellectual "Flintstones" enthusiast, "Flintstones" chess sets (below) were also available.

As an animated series designed for both adults and children, the broad appeal of the show greatly increased the range of products that the characters could endorse. Recognizing this potential, in 1969 Miles Laboratories developed a new product: children's vitamins that bore the likenesses of members of the Flintstone and Rubble families. Now manufactured in five varieties, Flintstones Vitamins continue to reign as the number one selling children's vitamin—a position they have held since they were introduced more than two decades ago.

When the Flintstones began endorsing breakfast cereals in 1971, Pebbles cereal was available, as it is today, in two flavors, fruity and cocoa. In 1991, Post added a new variety, Dino Pebbles—vanilla with marshmallows—but, lacking the success of its predecessors, it enjoyed only a limited run. Still, the original varieties have continued to be a smash hit in the breakfast food aisles, selling over sixty million boxes in 1992.

In addition to cereal and vitamins, a wide assortment of Flintstones merchandise was produced through the years, and with the show's continued popularity, new products are still being manufactured today. For the outdoor enthusiast there are inflatable kayaks and beach balls; for the couch potato, numerous videocassettes of classic episodes; and for the intellectual, the-Flintstones-meet-the-Jetsons chess sets are available as well. Die-hard Flintstones fans can attire themselves in Club Fred T-shirts, cook with Bedrock bakers' kits, and buy Modern Stone Age soap holders for the bathroom. And the true Flintstonephile can even pay for all these items with checks bearing the likenesses of the Flintstone family.

With all of the items available, one might get the impression that anyone can use the Flintstones to endorse their product, but this is not the case. Merchandisers must be licensed (over 500 companies currently hold that privilege), and an entire style guide has been developed to give licensees a guiding hand in illustrating the inhabitants of

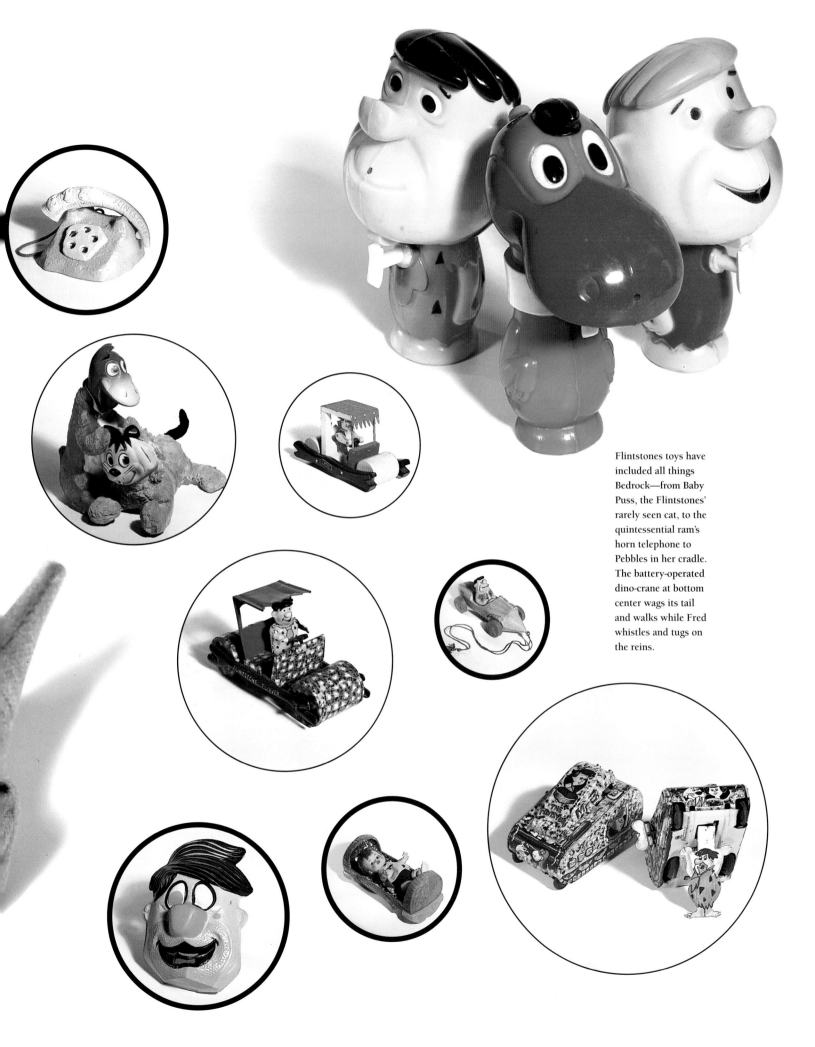

Flintstones toys have included all things Bedrock—from Baby Puss, the Flintstones' rarely seen cat, to the quintessential ram's horn telephone to Pebbles in her cradle. The battery-operated dino-crane at bottom center wags its tail and walks while Fred whistles and tugs on the reins.

Manufactured by Aladdin, the classic metal lunch box was the first of the "Flintstones" lunch line.

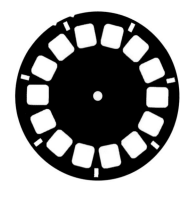

Long before the live-action movie, "The Flintstones" provided three-dimensional entertainment with Viewmaster reels (above and opposite). The figures were modeled out of clay and painstakingly photographed from two slightly different angles to create a stereoscopic effect.

Bedrock. Complete with model sheets for each character, the book demonstrates proper facial expressions for many of their moods—startled, angry, happy, perplexed—as well as the appropriate color schemes that must be followed to keep the characters true to their original likenesses.

Even armed with these guidelines, it can be easy to stray from a prehistoric mindset. Iwao Takamoto, who has given many seminars to prospective merchandisers teaching them the proper way to think Stone Age, brings up the example of an English T-shirt manufacturer. The company wanted Fred to ice skate in a winter scene and although Takamoto approved of dressing Fred in heavy layers of clothing, he balked at the company's design of Fred's ice skates. The T-shirt people had envisioned skates made of skins tied together to form a boot, but as Takamoto notes, the Flintstones rarely wear shoes. "Even in snow," he laughs, "they don't get cold and they don't seem to care or question it." Instead of boot-like skates, Takamoto suggested using a flat piece of wood with a tusk tied to it and two leather straps that would attach the contraption to Fred's bare foot.

In the early days of Flintstones merchandising, there was little control over the items being made, and a wide array of weird Bedrock characters was unleashed upon an unsuspecting world. Fred in a green suit, Barney with green hair, and a blue-bearded Fred with the misnomer "Rocky" are only a few of the stranger mutations that have appeared. "Some of those things are, in retrospect, quite delightful," Takamoto says, "because of a very strong primitive quality."

While this "off-model" memorabilia is highly prized by the collectors, they also consider everything "Flintstonian" worth accumulating. From premiums—the tiny toys that come inside cereal boxes as an incentive for purchase—to the cereal boxes themselves, a lucrative market exists for the hundreds of Flintstone products that have been manufactured over the years. Lunch boxes are currently among the most popular of the collectibles, costing far more than they did when they carried peanut butter-and-jelly sandwiches to the grade-school lunch table.

1 "I'll get to work on time using my invention."

2 "Ta! Ta! Wilma, I'm off to work the easy way."

7 on tim "Just Flints

Reel Two

THE FLINTSTO

GAF® VIEW-MASTER
Stereo Reel
PORTLAND, OREGON 97207
MADE IN U.S.A.

GAF CO
New Yo
T.M. Re
Marque De

in "Fred's Invent

"...made it time Boss!" - "Just barely, Flintstone."

Two

6

"Turn it off! TURN IT OFF!"

...TSTONES

GAF CORPORATION
New York, N.Y., U.S.A.
T.M. Reg. U.S. Pat. Off.
Marque Déposée Marca Reg.

"...Invention"

...oductions, Inc., 1962

142'

5

"Yeeoowww! Get out of the way," you dope!"

"Holy M...
Scran...
feath...
hitchhi...

4

Metal ones currently sell for between six hundred and one thousand dollars each. Another favorite find for the Flintstones collector is the Pebbles doll, the poppet that was marketed along with the birth of Pebbles in a campaign that still rates among the best in the business.

While the Flintstones Baby Contest is remembered by many fans, another Screen Gems promotion—this one featuring Hoppy, the Rubbles' pet hopparoo—seems to have faded quietly into the ether. For the 1965 contest that was held just for children, a song and dance, both called "The Hopparoo," were created. The country was divided into ten geographical regions with one zoo selected in each. A kangaroo at each of these zoos was designated the regional "hopparoo," and children were invited to send in their guesses as to how many hops the animal would make in a five hour period. The winning child in each region was flown to London for an International Hop-Off at the zoo in Regent's Park, with the winner receiving a grand prize of one thousand dollars to be used toward a college education.

Made into puppets, the cast of "The Flintstones" was available for the theatrically inclined viewer. Note the imaginative—although inaccurate designs: a bright green Hoppy with mule ears, a duck-billed Dino, and off-model costumes.

Wooden versions of Fred and Barney (left) were licensed by Hanna-Barbera, a characteristic that not all of the early "Flintstones" merchandise shared.

Digging deep into the Hanna-Barbera archives, researchers recently made a startling discovery—Fred Flintstone and Barney Rubble starred in an entire film devoted to the targeting of beer sales. Made specifically for Anheuser-Busch wholesalers and never presented to the public, the show wrapped a "Flintstones" cartoon around material devoted to the liquor company's advertising campaign for the year. In today's post-Stone Age world, it's difficult to imagine family-show characters extolling the virtues of alcoholic beverages, but in 1967 liquor advertising on television was perfectly acceptable.

Bartenders for a Day

The piece begins when Barney's dinosaur drops a slab of rock on Mr. Slate. He and Fred end up without jobs. Leaving the quarry, they stop at their favorite "tavern-type inn-bar-grill-lounge-pub-saloon" and retire to a table for a couple of rounds of Busch served in foamy mugs. Fred is upset from the showdown with Slate, but he magically calms down when a hand materializes out of thin air, pats him on the head, and purrs seductively, "Relax. Take it easy, tiger."

The next day, after being told by an employment agency counselor that they are qualified only for gravel pit engineering, the boys retire once again to the bar, where the barkeep leaves them to mind the store. Turning on the TV, they discover a "special advanced closed-circuit program for Anheuser-Busch wholesalers" and settle back to watch. After fifteen minutes of marketing strategy, the program ends and the bar fills with thirsty patrons.

The crowds eventually depart and Mr. Slate enters, disturbed because two of his key men quit. The magic hand materializes and strokes his bald pate. "Calm down, Slate honey," it says soothingly, "give them another chance."

Suddenly tranquil, Slate asks the "bartenders"—Fred and Barney in disguise—to help get his men back. They agree on the condition that Slate give the men a raise. When Slate refuses, Fred and Barney offer him a beer on the house. As he drinks, the hand materializes once again and purrs, "Be reasonable, tiger, you can afford them." Uncharacteristically, Slate agrees. As he swings happily out of the bar, he calls, "Good night, Fred and Barney—and don't be late in the morning."

Victorious, Fred and Barney pour themselves another Busch beer and shout in unison, "Yabba-Dabba-Doo!"

Don Garrett, Screen Gems' publicity director at the time, recalls the closed-circuit TV show that was sent to ABC affiliates to kick off the campaign. It featured Alan Reed, Mel Blanc, a bevy of dancing girls, and a rendition of the song performed by contemporary artists. "The funniest part of all," Garrett says, "was that we had a kangaroo, and it was the ugliest one I've ever seen in my life. It was not one of those smooth red kangaroos that we love from Australia. This was a woolly one with ugly gray fur, and as hard as we tried to get him to face the camera, every shot we had of him with Alan and Mel was always from the rear."

Dino, the Flintstone household counterpart to Hoppy, was rewarded by Post Cereals with his own promotion in 1988. The purple pet with a penchant for running away from home was said to have gone on vacation—somewhere between Mount Rushrock and Hollyrock—and children who helped locate him, via clues on boxes of Cocoa and Fruity Pebbles, became eligible for an all-expense paid trip to Hollywood.

But "The Flintstones" is recognized for far more than effective marketing campaigns. As Hanna-Barbera's biggest success story, the show is the company's cornerstone and an ongoing source of pride. The studio continues to focus on Fred Flintstone as spokesman and mascot, much as Mickey Mouse is for Disney. But that is nothing new. Fred and his family have always shone as stars. Much more than mere cartoon characters, they are a phenomenon. Their names are synonymous with breakfast cereals and vitamins, merchandise in which they are featured is sought after, and almost every man, woman, and child stopped on the street can rattle off at least part of their theme song. They have gracefully survived the ups and downs of thirty-four years of show business and are still going strong. In fact, they are as popular now as they were in the beginning of their careers.

Unique interpretations of Fred, Barney, and Dino; "Fred Flintstone's Bedrock Band," complete with tortoise shell cymbals and Fred playing a xylophone; Pebbles in a tortoise shell baby buggy; and a variety of "Flintstones" walking toys (clockwise from top, left).

In its first season, "The Flintstones" received an exceptional number of awards, including: Most Unique New Program, from Fame's Annual Critics' Poll; Most Original New Series, from the TV Radio Mirror; an Emmy nomination for Outstanding Achievement in the Field of Humor; and a Golden Globe award for Outstanding Achievement in International Television. And in the same year,

HANNA-BARBERA'S

THE FLINTSTONES

The very first "Flintstones" Little Golden Book was written before the show ever aired (opposite and below). In these early adventures Dino is called Harvey, and the little boy—who never actually appeared on the program—is named Junior.

Flintstones record albums abounded (above), providing listeners with a wide variety of musical themes. And for those more interested in reading than humming along, "Flintstones" comic books (below) offered adventures of another kind.

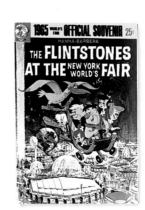

Jeff Rose, a Screen Gems publicity agent at the time of Pebble's "birth," says, "For a while I was known as the Dollman of Screen Gems. The Hanna-Barbera people gave me dozens and dozens of Pebbles dolls and I took them all over the country." Pebbles and Bamm-Bamm are packaged for the Spanish-speaking audience (above). Fred was also available as a hand-puppet, marionette, lamp, and TV antenna.

Bill Hanna and Joe Barbera were also honored with the prestigious Silver Plaque from the National Cartoonists' Society for their Flintstone animation efforts.

And that was only the beginning. TV Guide has since named "The Flintstones" their readers' choice for Best TV Cartoon, and the show's cast has gone on to garner accolades that normally are awarded only to actors of a more three-dimensional nature. *People* magazine listed Fred as one of the Top 25 Stars Over Fifty Years of Television, and not to be outdone by her husband, Wilma was named one of seven favorite TV moms by Universal Studios in Hollywood.

Wielding their tremendous public influence, the Flintstones have also been involved in many charitable causes. Big-hearted Fred has a soft spot for children and animals and this sentiment carries through to the agencies his family supports. Pebbles is the mascot of Operation Baby Buckle, helping to educate Americans on the importance of child safety seats and belts. Dino has helped foster awareness of the American Humane Society by appearing in special artwork. Fred and Wilma have represented the American Automobile Association's traffic safety awareness program, and along with the Rubbles, have participated in an Easter Seals dance marathon.

The Flintstones are the perfect representatives for these causes. With a universal appeal that crosses all age, cultural, and economic barriers, they are loved by millions of people around the world. An entire generation has grown up with the show and a new generation has already embarked upon a delightful intimacy with its characters. When Fred hollers "Yabba-Dabba-Doo!" it is recognized as an expression of joy not just for him but for everyone who loves "The Flintstones."

W hen Hanna-Barbera decided that the time had come for Fred and Wilma to have a baby, they had the good sense to call Don Garrett. Not an obstetrician, but the director of publicity for Screen Gems, the show's distributor, Garrett created a promotional strategy that at the time was one of the most successful in television history.

With the announcement of Wilma's pregnancy on an episode called, appropriately enough, "The Surprise," Garrett's office launched a full-scale media and marketing campaign. He recalls, "We sent press kits to all the ABC affiliates, providing slides, announcements, cute little articles, and so on." Newspapers and magazines across the country covered the story, and soon television viewers began to get drawn into the excitement.

Using on-air spots featuring a prehistoric stork, viewers were invited to send in postcards with the new baby's predicted weight in pounds and ounces. The first card drawn with the correct weight would win. The number of responses was astounding—over one million entries were submitted.

Pebbles's birth weight was determined to be six pounds, twelve ounces, and Garrett drew the winning card himself. "The winner, I recall, was a butcher from Florida," he says. "He and his wife got a trip around the world and a thousand dollars for expenses, which wasn't bad money in the early sixties.

"We also announced that any child born during the half-hour birth episode of 'The Flintstones' would win a twenty-five-dollar savings bond, as well as a Pebbles doll, conveniently fresh off the rack and stocked heavily at toy stores near you."

After the airing of the episode, titled "The Blessed Event," Garrett's staff was notified that over one hundred babies around the country had been born along with Pebbles. Station managers in each of these areas made hospital visits to the new arrivals and were photographed presenting the bond and the doll. "We got terrific press!" Garrett says triumphantly.

With all the publicity, doll sales skyrocketed, and so did ratings shares. Soon "The Flintstones" became the top-rated show in its time slot, adding three million homes to its viewership and pushing the chief competition, "Route 66" and "Sing Along with Mitch," into lower positions for weeks to come.

The Blessed Promotion

"The Flintstones" Episode Guide

very "Flintstones" fan remembers the landmark episodes—the birth of Pebbles, the time Stony Curtis came to stay, the day Fred and Barney sang with Ann-Margrock. But there are many others which are as fascinating, as quirky, and just as fun.

The typical "Flintstones" plot is fraught with substories, misunderstandings, and strange twists. Jewel thieves abound, as do cases of mistaken identity. Movie stars arrive in Bedrock with surprising frequency. When the Flintstones and Rubbles go on vacation, you can be sure trouble will follow. Fred and Barney quarrel and make up almost daily, and Mr. Slate seems to fire and rehire Fred on a whim.

Half the fun in watching "The Flintstones" is in seeing just how convoluted the story can get before its resolution. But whether you're watching the classic episodes for plot appeal or slapstick humor (just how many times has Fred gotten hit in the head with a bowling ball?), they always prove to be entertaining.

Here, then, for the trivia buff and die-hard historian alike, are detailed descriptions for each of the original 166 episodes—including production numbers, recording and air dates, story writers, and voice actors. While reviewing the episodes, the reader may note a lack of continuity between the shows' production numbers and their air dates. "The Flintstone Flyer," for example, while the first episode to be aired, was number two in order of production. The reason behind

this scheduling was that the studio felt "The Swimming Pool," production number one—in which Fred and Barney fight through the entire episode—was a poor choice with which to introduce the characters to the viewing audience. On other occasions, however, the reason why episodes aired when they did was arbitrary, having as much to do with which animation unit finished production first (there were several units working at one time) as with anything else. Additionally, some shows were simply produced out of sequence. "Daddies Anonymous"—in which Barney and Fred join a fathers' club—is listed as production number 98, while "Little Bamm-Bamm"—in which Barney's son makes his first appearance—is number 101. This was not a problem as long as the shows were aired in sequence. But to further complicate matters, the final decision on when to broadcast the episodes ultimately rested with the network, which had its own scheduling ideas.

THE SWIMMING POOL

1

Production No.: P-1
Story: Warren Foster
Recording Date: 4/1/60
Air Date: 10/14/60

Voices:

Alan Reed	Fred, Sergeant
Mel Blanc	Barney, Cop, Clerk
Jean Vander Pyl	Wilma
Bea Benaderet	Betty
Mike Rye	Charlie, Guy, Announcer, 2nd Guy
Daws Butler	Cop

Trouble starts when Fred and Barney decide to become partners in building a backyard swimming pool. After Barney throws a party, Fred gets mad and fences off half the pool. In retaliation, Barney removes half the water. Then Barney throws another party and Fred sends a friend, who is impersonating a cop, to quell the bash. When Fred discovers the party is in celebration of his birthday, he and Barney make up. Meanwhile, the real police arrive and arrest Fred for disturbing the peace. All's well that ends well, however, with the boys friends again, declaring, "Our friendship is written in water—pool water, that is." In this charter episode, Fred hollers, "Yahoo!" instead of the not-yet-coined "Yabba dabba doo!"

THE FLINTSTONE FLYER

2

Production No.: P-2
Story: Mike Maltese
Recording Date: 4/2/60
Air Date: 9/30/60

Voices:

Alan Reed	Fred
Mel Blanc	Barney
Jean Vander Pyl	Wilma
Bea Benaderet	Betty

Fred feigns illness so he and Barney can go bowling instead of to the opera with their wives. Betty and Wilma head to the theater while Barney stays behind to nurse Fred, and as soon as the girls are gone, the boys soar off to the bowling alley in Barney's homemade helicopter. During intermission, the wives go to the bowling alley to call home and they spot their errant husbands. Sighting their wives, Fred and Barney fashion moustache disguises out of broom bristles and race for home in the copter, hoping to beat the girls. They make it in time, but unfortunately Barney forgets to remove his moustache. Escaping to the skies, the boys pedal furiously in the copter, while the irate girls sit outside in the starlight, waiting for them to run out of steam. It is in this milestone episode that Fred first yells, "Yabba dabba doo!"

THE PROWLER

3

Production No.: P-3
Story: Joseph Barbera
Recording Date: 4/5/60
Air Date: 12/30/60

Voices:

Alan Reed	Fred
Mel Blanc	Barney, Rockymoto
Jean Vander Pyl	Wilma
Bea Benaderet	Betty
Maxie Rosenbloom	Crook

With a burglar on the loose in Bedrock, Betty signs up for a judo course with Professor Rockymoto. Wilma wants to enroll, too, but Fred claims that judo or not, at the first sign of a prowler, Betty would hide under the bed. To prove it, he climbs in the Rubbles' window during the night. Betty demonstrates her judo and throws him out. Meanwhile, the real prowler is at the Flintstone home and so is Fred in his prowler mask. Wilma throws them both to the floor with judo that she learned from Betty. When the bonafide burglar comes back for his loot, they all take refuge under the bed. The show ends with everyone taking judo lessons—including the prowler.

THE BABYSITTERS

4

Production No.: P-4
Story: Warren Foster
Recording Date: 4/6/60
Air Date: 11/11/60

Voices:

Alan Reed	Fred
Mel Blanc	Barney
Jean Vander Pyl	Wilma
Bea Benaderet	Betty
Daws Butler	Fight Announcer, Fireman, Bill, Joe Granite, Sergeant, Lester

Fred and Barney are deputized as babysitters for little Egbert while his mother, Edna, plays bridge with the girls. Taking the tyke to Joe Rockhead's to watch the fights on TV seems like a good idea, but when Egbert dresses Joe's runtosaurus in his clothes, everything goes haywire. The pooch escapes out the window, and Fred and Barney give chase thinking it's Egbert. Then Joe comes home and thinks his house has been burgled. He calls the police and everybody, including the baby, ends up in the slammer.

THE ENGAGEMENT RING

5

Production No.: P-5
Story: Warren Foster
Recording Date: 4/8/60
Air Date: 11/25/60

Voices:

Alan Reed	Fred, Champ
Mel Blanc	Barney, Garbage man, Fight manager
Jean Vander Pyl	Wilma, Little girl
Bea Benaderet	Betty, Edna, Little boy

Big-hearted Barney buys a belated engagement ring for Betty and gives it to Fred to hide until he presents it. Wilma discovers the ring in Fred's favorite hiding place—his bowling ball—and thinks it's meant for her. Afraid to tell her the truth, Fred cons Barney into going three minutes in the ring with the champ for a $500 purse that would provide funds to replace the diamond. When the girls find out, they pay the champ to throw the fight. He doesn't and poor Barney gets flattened. When an irate Wilma then flattens the champ, she and Betty go home with both the $500 they paid to throw the fight and the $500 purse, enough to pay for diamonds for both wives.

NO HELP WANTED

6

Production No.: P-6
Story: Warren Foster
Recording Date: 4/11/60
Air Date: 10/21/60

Voices:

Alan Reed	Fred
Mel Blanc	Barney, Salesman, Dog
Jean Vander Pyl	Wilma
Bea Benaderet	Betty, Little boy
Frank Nelson	Boulder, Rocky Stone

After getting Barney fired from his job, Fred feels bad and uses his influence to get his friend a new one. Barney's new career is as a furniture repo man (his oath: Neither rain nor snow nor threats of tears will keep this collector from the completion of his contemptible duty), and his first task is to take back Fred's TV set. After several disastrous attempts to wrest the TV from Fred's grasp, Barney finally runs away with it. He feels so bad, though, that he takes an advance on his first week's pay to bail out the TV. Fred's all smiles—until he learns that Barney's next assignment is to repossess his golf clubs. This episode marks Dino's first appearance as a member of the Flintstone family.

AT THE RACES

7

Production No.: P-7
Story: Syndey Zelinka
Recording Date: 4/18/60
Air Date: 11/18/60

Voices:

Alan Reed	Fred
Mel Blanc	Barney, Crook, Doc, Monkey sounds
Jean Vander Pyl	Wilma
Hal Smith	P.A. announcer, Dan, Boxx, Colonel, Seller, Dinosaur yawn

Determined to buy Boulder Dan's billiard parlor and become a businessman, Fred tries to get the necessary cash by betting his pay on a longshot at the dinosaur track. To play it safe, he and Barney tell Wilma that the paycheck has been stolen. When the long shot, Sabre Tooth, actually wins—by his rider's nose—Fred and Barney are wild with joy. But when they go to retrieve their winnings, which they have temporarily hidden under a rock, poor Fred is robbed and beaten, and loving wife Wilma doesn't believe a word of the story.

THE DRIVE-IN

8

Production No.: P-8
Story: Warren Foster
Recording Date: 4/25/60
Air Date: 12/23/60

Voices:

Alan Reed	Fred
Mel Blanc	Barney
Jean Vander Pyl	Wilma
Bea Benaderet	Betty
Hal Smith	Man, Butcher, Patron, Announcer
Jinny Tyler	Daisy
Nancy Wible	Gwen

Fred and Barney buy a drive-in diner without telling their wives. Having few customers but a couple of cute dancing carhops for employees, the boys are having a blast, until their wives show up wearing carhop uniforms and furious expressions. They make the boys go back to their old jobs, and to celebrate, all four go to dinner at the Rockadero, where Wilma and Betty entertain everyone with their version of the carhop can-can.

HOT LIPS HANNIGAN

9

Production No.: P-9
Story: Warren Foster
Recording Date: 5/2/60
Air Date: 10/7/60

Voices:

Alan Reed	Fred
Mel Blanc	Barney, 2nd Voice, Shelly
Jean Vander Pyl	Wilma, Zaza, 3rd Girl
Bea Benaderet	Betty, Dressmaker, 1st Girl, 2nd Girl
Jerry Mann	1st Voice, Hot Lips

Practicing with magician's paraphernalia for the Lodge show, Fred makes Wilma and Betty "disappear." Believing their wives have really vanished, he and Barney head for the local dance hall, the Rockland, where an old friend, Hot Lips Hannigan, is playing with his band. Betty and Wilma—who staged their disappearance—don disguises and follow. With Fred singing and Barney on drums, the pair are having a high time—and wowing the young, hip crowd—until they become too popular and have to run from the adoring kids. Betty and Wilma, still in disguise, accost them at home and fear Fred, not recognizing Wilma and fearing his wife will find he's been the object of a fan's affections, faints.

THE SPLIT PERSONALITY

10

Production No.: P-10
Story: Warren Foster
Recording Date: 5/9/60
Air Date: 10/28/60

Voices:

Alan Reed	Fred, 1st Man
Mel Blanc	Barney, Bird, 3rd Man, Announcer
Jean Vander Pyl	Wilma
Bea Benaderet	Betty
Howard McNear	Doctor

When Fred accidentally conks himself on the head with a bottle, he undergoes a bizzare character change. Regaining consciousness as Frederick, he becomes an aristocratic highbrow who disrupts the status quo of Bedrock with his sophisticated manners and tastes. His bowling pals form the "Get Rid of Frederick or Else Club," and Barney decides the only cure is to conk Fred on the head again. Neither he, Wilma, nor Betty is willing to be the conker, so Barney sets up a rock to fall from a doorway when Fred opens it. The trick works and good ol' loud-mouthed Fred is back.

THE SNORKASAURUS HUNTER

11

Production No.: P-11
Story: Warren Foster, Mike Maltese
Recording Date: N/A
Air Date: 1/27/61

Voices:

Alan Reed	Fred
Mel Blanc	Barney, Bird, Mosquito
Jean Vander Pyl	Wilma
Bea Benaderet	Betty, Kid
Jerry Mann	Ed, Butch, Cop, Snorkasaurus

To save on the high cost of groceries, the Flintstones and Rubbles go camping, where Fred plans to hunt for his food. While Wilma and Betty remain at the tent site, the boys go off in search of a snorkasaurus, armed with a golf bag full of numbered clubs. The snorkasaurus, a big, blue dinosaur with a flamboyant personality, takes refuge with the girls, and when the boys go after it, Wilma defends him. Before Fred and Barney know what's happened, the snorkasaurus has come home with them and is happily cleaning, ironing, and answering the phone. In a confusing twist at the end of the episode, Wilma calls him Dino.

HOLLYROCK, HERE I COME

12

Production No.: P-12
Story: Warren Foster
Recording Date: 5/20/60
Air Date: 12/2/60

Voices:

Alan Reed	Fred, Pilot
Mel Blanc	Barney, Bird, Co-pilot, Assistant Producer
Jean Vander Pyl	Wilma
Bea Benaderet	Betty
Jerry Mann	Announcer, Man, Plane announcer, Producer

When Wilma and Betty win a trip to Hollyrock with their TV slogan contest entry, they excitedly depart to hobnob with the stars. Left behind in Bedrock, the boys soon get bored and fly out to join them. When they find Wilma rehearsing for the television epic, "The Frogmouth," and playing the part of a "real wife with an overbearing, loud-mouthed husband," Fred is quickly cast as the husband. Stardom quickly goes to Fred's head, but when the TV cameras start to turn, he loses his voice. After the Flintstones and Rubbles have been home for a week, Fred still can't speak—until, that is, Wilma goes out and buys a $5,000 fur coat.

THE GIRLS' NIGHT OUT

 13

Production No.: P-13

Story: Warren Foster

Recording Date: 5/31/60

Air Date: 1/6/61

Voices:

Alan Reed	Fred
Mel Blanc	Barney, Colonel
Jean Vander Pyl	Wilma
Bea Benaderet	Betty, 2nd Girl
Jerry Mann	Boss, Announcer, 2nd Boy
Nancy Russell	1st Girl, 3rd Girl, Kid, Bird

At the amusement park, Fred cuts a record in a do-it-yourself recording booth but accidentally leaves it behind. A group of teens picks it up and falls in love with the "unknown troubador." When the Keen Teen Record Company plays it on the radio, Wilma calls to say it's Fred's voice, and the promoter shows up to transform Fred into Hi-Fye, teen idol. He attires him in cool skins, glasses (to appeal to eggheads), parts his hair down the middle, and sends the Flintstones and Rubbles out on tour where Fred is a smash hit. Wilma and Betty grow exhausted with life on the road, but the promoter tells them to be patient; teens are fickle, he says, and Fred's star will wane soon enough. The girls decide to speed things along by spreading an ugly rumor about Hi-Fye—the worst word in the teen language—that he's a square. It leaps from kid to kid, and soon Fred is playing to an empty room.

THE MONSTER FROM THE TAR PITS

 14

Production No.: P-14

Story: Warren Foster

Recording Date: 6/22/60

Air Date: 11/4/60

Voices:

Alan Reed	Fred, Ad Lib Voice
Mel Blanc	Barney, Pelican, Airport announcer
Jean Vander Pyl	Wilma, Ad lib voice
Bea Benaderet	Betty, Announcer
Bob Hopkins	Sandstone, Gary Granite
Jerry Mann	Director

Gullible Fred sees plenty of stars when he becomes actor Gary Granite's stand-in for the film "Monster From the Tar Pits." The director tells Fred he'll divide the part between him and Granite and has both actors costumed in purple monster suits. But it's Fred who gets hit with a real boulder and real clubs (fakes are too expensive), and an improvised ending (writers are too expensive) that requires him to stay submerged in a tar pit for half an hour—long after the movie company has packed up and left.

THE GOLF CHAMPION

 15

Production No.: P-15

Story: Sydney Zelinka

Recording Date: 6/29/60

Air Date: 12/9/60

Voices:

Alan Reed	Fred
Mel Blanc	Barney, Snore, Bird, Dog, Monkey
Jean Vander Pyl	Wilma
Bea Benaderet	Betty, 2nd Bird
John Stephenson	Announcer, Chairman, Guy, Charlie, 1st Guy

Winning the Lodge golf tournament, Fred declares "cold war" on club president Barney for withholding his trophy. Barney stubbornly counters with "no dues, no trophy," claiming that Fred owes the club a month's fees. The animosity mounts until Wilma and Betty start Operation Buddy Buddy, paying Barney the back dues and presenting Fred with the cup.

THE SWEEPSTAKES TICKET

 16

Production No.: P-16

Story: Warren Foster

Recording Date: 7/11/60

Air Date: 12/16/60

Voices:

Alan Reed	Fred, Good Angel
Mel Blanc	Barney, Dog, 1st Cop
Jean Vander Pyl	Wilma
Bea Benaderet	Betty, Mrs.R.
John Stephenson	Charlie, Old Man, Sergeant, Radio announcer

Confusion reigns when the husbands and wives buy two separate sweepstakes tickets and hide them from each other. Barney hides the boys' ticket in an old coat that Betty subsequently gives to a passing tramp. Discovering the loss in the nick of time, Barney apprehends the tramp (who sounds strangely like W. C. Fields), reappropriates the ticket, and hides it in the Rubbles' cookie jar. Meanwhile, Betty has hidden the girls' ticket in a coffee pot on the same kitchen shelf. Goaded by an angel and a devil, both of whom look like Fred himself, Fred decides to follow his more devilish impulse. He sneaks into the Rubble house and accidentally takes the girls' ticket—which later turns out to be the winning one. Egged on by their respective devils, the boys gleefully plan to spend all the money and drive away, yelling "Chaaarge it!"

THE HYPNOTIST

17

Production No.: P-17

Story: Warren Foster

Recording Date: 7/25/60

Air Date: 2/10/61

Voices:

Alan Reed	Fred, Subject
Mel Blanc	Barney, 2nd Subject, Bird, Clerk, Cat, Dog, Dog catcher
Jean Vander Pyl	Wilma, Woman
Bea Benaderet	Betty, Nurse
Howard McNear	Doctor
Jerry Mann	Announcer, 2nd Announcer, Mesmo, Cashier, Usher

When Wilma and Betty watch a TV program starring Mesmo, a hypnotist, Fred decides to demonstrate his own hypnotizing skills on his wife. His technique fails on her but puts Barney under completely, leaving him thinking he's a dog. Shaken, Fred takes his pal to the vet, who has trouble acknowledging that Barney is anything other than a healthy pet. Barney then gets picked up by the dog catcher and put in the pound. Fred goes to the TV station to consult Mesmo—who's busy dehypnotizing members of the studio audience—and brings him to the pound. Mesmo succeeds in returning Barney to normal, but leaves behind two dogs who think they're human.

THE HOT PIANO

18

Production No.: P-18

Story: Mike Maltese

Recording Date: 7/27/60

Air Date: 2/3/61

Voices:

Alan Reed	Fred
Mel Blanc	Barney, Lizard
Jean Vander Pyl	Wilma
Bea Benaderet	Betty
Frank Nelson	Clerk
Daws Butler	Con Man, Postman, Cop, Sergeant

For their anniversary, Fred decides to buy Wilma a piano from 88 Fingers Louie, a salesman who operates on a cash and U-carry basis from the back of a truck. After Fred and Barney lug the genuine Stoneway home and hide it in the garage until Wilma is asleep, they spend a laborious late night trying to get it into the house. The piano escapes from their grasp and begins speeding down the street with Fred aboard. Fred is arrested by the police, who think he's 88 Fingers. The desk sergeant lets him go home when he realizes that it's his anniversary, too, and he has to get a gift for his wife. The piano is brought into Fred and Wilma's bedroom, and with Barney at the keyboard, all the cops serenade Wilma with "Happy Anniversary" sung to the tune of the William Tell Overture. When the song ends, Fred and the piano are hauled out to the paddy wagon. Just as they are about to be driven away, word comes in that 88 Fingers has confessed to the crime.

THE BIG BANK ROBBERY

19

Production No.: P-19

Story: Arthur Phillips

Recording Date: 8/15/60

Air Date: 1/20/61

Voices:

Alan Reed	Fred, Looie, Benny
Mel Blanc	Barney, 1st Cop, Bird
Jean Vander Pyl	Wilma
Bea Benaderet	Betty, Mama Eagle
John Stephenson	Fingers, Sarge, Announcer, Attendant

Fred's daydreams of wealth become a reality—temporarily—when a couple of bank robbers on the lam toss a bag containing $86,000 into the Rubbles' yard. Forced by Betty and Wilma to return the money to the bank, the boys are en route when they are mistaken for the crooks. On the lam themselves, they drop off the dough at the Flintstone residence and hide out in the woods. Meanwhile, Wilma and Betty, gussied up as gun molls, head for the Poiple Dinosaur, a dive of a bar, to try a Stone Age sting and nab the real robbers. Worrying that their wives are at home with the loot unprotected, the boys sneak back, just as the robbers arrive with Betty and Wilma. Barney enters the Flintstone house, and while Fred waits in the car, he and the girls are tied up by the crooks. Growing anxious, Fred opens his front door—violently as usual—and slams the crooks behind it, saving the day.

ARTHUR QUARRY'S DANCE CLASS

20

Production No.: P-20

Story: Warren Foster

Recording Date: 8/22/60

Air Date: 1/13/61

Voices:

Alan Reed	Fred, 2nd Voice, 2nd Fireman
Mel Blanc	Barney, Dino, 1st Voice, Bird, 3rd Voice, 1st Fireman
Jean Vander Pyl	Wilma, Sabrina Gravel
Bea Benaderet	Betty, Venus Pitchblend
John Stephenson	Mailman, Joe Rockhead

Fred and Barney attempt to teach themselves ballroom dancing from a library book. When Barney throws out his back with a particularly arduous move, they enroll at the Arthur Quarry Dance School. To get out of the house every night for the week of the lessons, they join Joe Rockhead's Volunteer Fire Department, which raises a mock alert every evening at 7:30. Suspicious, Betty and Wilma call in and report a fire, and Joe rouses his men to action. Fred and Barney are not among the firefighters, and when the girls threaten to call the other wives, Joe confesses that their husbands are at Arthur Quarry's. Furious, Betty and Wilma show up at the class, only to learn the boys have been practicing for them.

LOVE LETTERS ON THE ROCKS

21

Production No.: P-21
Story: Arthur Phillips
Recording Date: 9/2/60
Air Date: 2/17/61

Voices:

Alan Reed	Fred
Mel Blanc	Barney, Dino,
	Cabbie, Bartender
Jean Vander Pyl	Wilma
Bea Benaderet	Betty, Brigette
John Stephenson	Perry Gunite,
	Jeweler

Fred's world crumbles when he finds a love poem addressed to Wilma. After reading lines like, "Your shell-like ears, your dainty hands, Your eyes so black, like frying pans," Fred goes nuts and hires a private detective, Perry Gunite, a cool dude with a Cary Grant voice and a hip strut. On the case, Gunite discovers Barney alone with Wilma and snaps a picture. What neither Perry nor Fred realizes is that Barney was pleading with Wilma to give up her affair. And what none of them realizes is that Fred was actually the author of the poem, it being one of many he penned in high school. When Fred learns the truth, he begs for Wilma's forgiveness on bended knee.

THE TYCOON

22

Production No.: P-22
Story: Warren Foster
Recording Date: 9/13/60
Air Date: 2/24/61

Voices:

Alan Reed	Fred, 2nd Man,
	J. L. Gotrocks
Mel Blanc	Barney, Guy, G. W.,
	Polly, Doorman
Jean Vander Pyl	Wilma,
	Ad Lib Voice
Bea Benaderet	Betty, Secretary
John Stephenson	Narrator, F. M.,
	Boss, 2nd Guy,
	Stonehead,
	Owner, Man

When Fred Flintstone look-alike, tycoon J. L. Gotrocks, runs away from his office to "mingle with the real people," Fred is commandeered by Gotrocks executives to impersonate the tycoon. If he refuses, the execs plead, "Widows and babies will lose their life savings; the whole country will go broke . . . and besides we'll lose our cinchy jobs." Fred agrees and soon finds himself surrounded by ringing phones and clamoring board members. Meanwhile, Gotrocks is enjoying the simple life in Fred's old haunts, playing pinball and pool. When Wilma and the Rubbles find Gotrocks, they believe him to be Fred, and try to reason with him. He body slams Barney and calls his wife (they think he means Wilma) a battle-axe. Before long, each man is fed up with his new life, and both run away—Fred from the executives, Gotrocks from Wilma and the Rubbles. The tycoon is finally trapped by the executives in an ashcan, and Fred returns home to face a furious wife and neighbors.

THE ASTR'NUTS

23

Production No.: P-23
Story: Warren Foster
Recording Date: 9/27/60
Air Date: 3/3/61

Voices:

Alan Reed	Fred, Professor
Mel Blanc	Barney, Mortar, Animal,
	Doctor, Foreman,
	Platoon Sergeant,
	3rd Guy, 1st Voice
Jean Vander Pyl	Wilma
Bea Benaderet	Betty
John Stephenson	Charlie, 1st Sarge,
	General, Announcer,
	2nd Guy
Jerry Mann	Guy, Bilko Sarge, 1st
	Guy, 2nd Voice

Under the impression they are being examined for a physical fitness contest, Fred and Barney blunder into three year Army enlistments. Reluctantly reporting to Camp Millstone, they find themselves in the charge of a bespectacled sergeant who sets them up for an assignment that's so top secret he can't tell them about it. It turns out to be a trip to the moon via Stone Age rocket—a sling-shot-launched sawed-off log with a pointed tip. Long before they reach the ionosphere, the rocket returns them to Earth where they're hailed as heroes and let out of the service.

THE LONG, LONG WEEKEND

24

Production No.: P-24
Story: Warren Foster
Recording Date: 10/24/60
Air Date: 3/10/61

Voices:

Alan Reed	Fred, Voice
Mel Blanc	Barney, Poobah
Jean Vander Pyl	Wilma, 1st Voice,
	2nd Voice
Bea Benaderet	Betty, Woman,
	Phone woman
Willard	Gus

Fred's old pal, "Smoothie" Gus, invites the Flintstones and Rubbles for a free vacation at his seaside hotel, neglecting to mention that all the help has quit. Before long, Fred is working as the chef, Barney as the bellboy, and the girls as maids. When a Water Buffalo convention descends upon the hotel, the Flintstones and Rubbles decide to leave and the Grand Poobah volunteers the Women's Auxiliary to fill all the employment positions. Fred and Barney are impressed with his power—until the women riot, breaking up the chairs and sending the Poobah running for his life.

IN THE DOUGH

25

Production No.: P-25
Story: Arthur Phillips
Recording Dates: 11/12/60
and 11/17/60
Air Date: 3/17/61

Voices:

Alan Reed	Fred
Mel Blanc	Barney, Duck Bird, Charlie, Dino
Jean Vander Pyl	Wilma
Bea Benaderet	Betty
Hal Smith	Sponsor, Announcer

Wilma and Betty are chosen as finalists in the Tasty Pastry bake-off contest for their Flint Rubble Double Bubble Cake. But when they come down with measles an hour before the plane leaves, Fred and Barney, unwilling to give up the chance for the $10,000 purse, decide to fill in. Attired in wigs and dresses, "Mrs. Flintstone" and "Mrs. Rubble" win the grand prize—until Barney displays a rival flour brand as the vital ingredient on national TV and is hauled off the stage in disgrace.

THE GOOD SCOUT

26

Production No.: P-26
Story: Warren Foster
Recording Date: 11/12/60
Air Date: 3/24/61

Voices:

Alan Reed	Fred
Mel Blanc	Barney, Conductor, Dino, Sheep, Bear
Jean Vander Pyl	Wilma, Scout
Bea Benaderet	Betty, Scout
Hal Smith	Radio announcer
Lucille Bliss	Hugo, Scout

When Fred assumes command of a Boy Scout troop, he quickly learns the hazards of the great outdoors. Traipsing through Granite Canyon, he comes face-to-face with a saber-toothed bear. Fred tells Barney to escape with the boys while he leads the animal away. When Barney tells him to play dead, he does—and the bear throws him over a cliff. Later, after pitching their tent on a log platform in a rain storm, Fred, Barney, and the boys are cozy and snug. In the morning though, they discover they're floating on a river, headed straight for a waterfall. Thinking quickly, Fred has the boys tie the tent's corners together to form a parachute. They all float off the endangered raft but get caught on a tree limb over the raging falls. After they are rescued by a ranger and returned home, the scouts award Fred a plaque in thanks.

ROOMS FOR RENT

27

Production No.: P-27
Story: Warren Foster
Recording Date: 1/11/61
Air Date: 3/31/61

Voices:

Alan Reed	Fred, Guard
Mel Blanc	Barney, Bird, Kid, Dino, Conductor, 1st Monkey
Jean Vander Pyl	Wilma, Kid
Bea Benaderet	Betty, Kid
Daws Butler	2nd Monkey, 1st Guy
Don Messick	2nd Guy, Emcee

Betty and Wilma decide to bring in a little extra money by renting their guest rooms. Their first takers are a pair of music students from Bedrock College who can't afford to both pay rent and buy records, so the girls make a deal—the students will get two weeks room and board in exchange for coaching Wilma and Betty for their upcoming Lodge show act. Before long, with one boarder pounding the piano at the Rubbles' and the other banging the bongos at the Flintstones', Fred and Barney are fit to be tied. But when the girls win the contest and the grand prize of $500, they return home to find their husbands earnestly practicing for next year's show.

FRED FLINTSTONE— BEFORE AND AFTER

28

Production No.: P-28
Story: Warren Foster
Recording Date: 1/23/61
Air Date: 4/7/61

Voices:

Alan Reed	Fred
Mel Blanc	Barney, Dino, Slabsides
Jean Vander Pyl	Wilma, Girl
Bea Benaderet	Betty, Receptionist
John Stephenson	Boss, Guy, Al, 3rd Guy, Frank
Hal Smith	Cop, 2nd Guy, Charlie, Man
Bern Bennett	Announcer, Speaker

When Fred costars in a before and after weight loss commercial for Fat Off Reducing Method, he's convinced he's the "after" half of the team, conveniently forgetting that he was the one the announcer called "all lard." Wilma drags him down to the station to make them pull the insulting commercial off the air, but instead, Fred is coerced into losing twenty-five pounds in a month for a $1,000 prize. Poor Fred has a hard time dieting, and the fact that Wilma and the Rubbles boobytrap the refrigerators has no effect. In desperation, he joins Food Anonymous, whose loyal members keep him true to his diet, stealing every bite before it gets into his mouth. When he wins the challenge, Fred rushes to the phone and calls the club to resign, but their tactics continue unabated.

DROOP ALONG FLINTSTONE

29 Production No.: P-29
Story: Warren Foster
Recording Date: 1/30/61
Air Date: 9/22/61

Voices:

Alan Reed	Fred, Voices, Fred
Daws Butler	Barney, Director, Voices
Jean Vander Pyl	Wilma
Bea Benaderet	Betty, Mary Lou Jim
Hal Smith	Tumble, Manager, Attendant, Bronk, Chet
John Stephenson	Driver, Maitre d', Guy, Chuck, Voices, Indian

On a visit to Bedrock, Cousins Tumbleweed and Mary Lou Jim ask Fred and Wilma to take care of their ranch while they go on a trip. The Rubbles join the Flintstones and they arrive at their destination unaware that a Hollyrock film company is shooting nearby. When Fred and Barney stumble into the filming of a saloon brawl in a ghost town, the director—who doesn't shoot scenes more than once on his low budget—writes the boys into the script. Movie Indians chase the intrepid pair, who think they're real and run for their lives. The "Indians" tie them to stakes and perform a war dance, but soon are running for their own lives when Betty and Wilma arrive to save their husbands.

FRED FLINTSTONE WOOS AGAIN

30 Production No.: P-30
Story: Jack Raymond
Recording Date: 2/7/61
Air Date: 10/13/61

Voices:

Alan Reed	Fred
Daws Butler	Barney, Dino, Animal, Stonewall, Guy, Rocky
Jean Vander Pyl	Wilma
Bea Benaderet	Betty
Frank Nelson	Clerk

On a second honeymoon at Rock Mountain Inn, Fred and Wilma decide to renew their vows at the combination coffee shop and chapel—the second ceremony and second cup are free. When they learn that Judge Wedrock was never legally licensed to marry them the first time, Wilma decides to make Fred prove his love by wooing her all over again. Fred refuses to go along, so Wilma incites his jealousy by offering Barney his bowling ball and ordering five pounds of rock candy delivered to her door. Fred finally gives in and professes his love. Later, the couple discovers that the first ceremony was not illegal after all.

THE HIT SONG WRITERS

31 Production No.: P-31
Story: Jack Raymond
Recording Date: 2/7/61
Air Date: 9/15/61

Voices:

Alan Reed	Fred
Daws Butler	Barney, Cuckoo, Small Rooster, Big Rooster, Welk
Jean Vander Pyl	Wilma, Baby, Librarian, Teenager
Bea Benaderet	Betty, Girl, Mabel
John Stephenson	Scat, Rockwell
Hoagy Carmichael	Hoagy

Fred discovers that Barney is a poet and decides they'll go into business as songwriters. Consulting a library book, *There's Loot in Lyrics*, for tips, they plan to pen a song containing all the elements people like—happiness, sadness, mothers, and with words like hooba-rooba. After an all night session, they come up with a sure-fire hit and pay Scat Von Rocktoven to write the music. They take their new song to music publisher Roland Rockwell, where they run into Hoagy Carmichael (voiced by himself), who volunteers to play for their audition. It turns out that Von Rocktoven is a crook and the music he "wrote" for their original gem is actually Hoagy's own "Stardust." Nevertheless, Rockwell falls in love with a song he finds in Fred and Barney's briefcase, "Yabba Dabba Dabba Dabba Doo," and commissions Hoagy to write a melody for it. At the best supper club in town in the posh Piltdown Hotel, Hoagy plays and sings their tune.

THE ROCK QUARRY STORY

32 Production No.: P-32
Story: Warren Foster
Recording Date: 2/24/61
Air Date: 10/20/61

Voices:

Alan Reed	Fred
Daws Butler	Barney, B. L., 2nd man
Jean Vander Pyl	Wilma, Crowd, 2nd and 4th voices
Bea Benaderet	Betty, Crowd, Girl, 1st and 3rd voices
John Stephenson	Rock Quarry, Man
Bob Hopkins	Gary, Charlie

Hollyrock hunk Rock Quarry arrives in Bedrock and decides to resume his pre-fame name and station in life. As simple Gus Schultz, he is invited home for dinner by Fred. When Wilma recognizes him, she literally bounces off the wall, but Rock insists he's not a movie star. When Betty also recognizes him as Quarry, he maintains his fictional guise as good ol' Gus. After a bout of bowling with Fred and Barney, however, Rock decides he does miss his old life. The only trouble is, now he can't get anyone to believe he really is a star and his efforts to prove it cause Fred to throw him out of the house. When Betty and Wilma learn his true identity, they throw Fred and Barney out of the house, into the pool. Then when Gary Granite comes calling, the girls tie him up so he can't get away.

THE LITTLE WHITE LIE

33

Production No.: P-33
Story: Herb Finn
Recording Date: 3/23/61
Air Date: 11/10/61

Voices:

Alan Reed	Fred, Pressman
Daws Butler	Barney, Porcupine, Clerk, Cop, Cabby
Jean Vander Pyl	Wilma
Bea Benaderet	Betty, Boy
John Stephenson	Stan, Sam, Mac, Man, Voice
Sandra Gould	Daisy

Winning $200 in a poker game proves to be a problem for Fred—he told Wilma he was going to visit a sick friend. When he convinces her that he found the money, she runs an ad in the paper to locate the owner. Fred has Barney pretend to be Mrs. Tillie Shimmelstone, the owner, and have the money mailed to the post office marked general delivery. Discovered by the girls with the loot, Fred tells Wilma and Betty that the money is Barney's. The two couples then celebrate "Barney's" money with a night out on the town, and Fred grumpily counts every penny spent, much to the girls' confusion.

THE SOFT TOUCHABLES

34

Production No.: P-34
Story: Sydney Zelinka/ Arthur Phillips
Recording Date: 4/9/61
Air Date: 10/27/61

Voices:

Alan Reed	Fred
Mel Blanc	Barney
Jean Vander Pyl	Wilma
Bea Benaderet	Betty
Sandra Gould	Dagmar
Daws Butler	1st Guy, 2nd Guy, Knuckles, Sarge
John Stephenson	Voice, Boss, Announcer, Cop

Trying to break into the private eye business, Fred and Barney eagerly—but not too wisely—take on Dagmar, the peroxide kid, as their first client. The blonde baddie takes them to Boss Rockhead, a notorious criminal posing as a bank president, who hires them to "stand guard" while he and his cohort, Knuckles, blow open the bank (he tells them he forgot his key) and transport the money to a safe place. After the job, the thieves kidnap Fred and Barney in a taxi and drive off with them to a fate fraught with cement mixers. When Wilma and Betty come upon the quartet in the middle of the road, fixing a flat, Barney knocks the bad guys flat with the bad tire and the girls follow up with handbag bashes. Fred and Barney are named heroes in the newspaper and the girls decide to become private eyes, too.

FLINTSTONE OF PRINSTONE

35

Production No.: P-35
Story: Larry Markes
Recording Date: 4/10/61
Air Date: 11/3/61

Voices:

Alan Reed	Fred, Quagmire, Crowd
Mel Blanc	Barney, Turtle, Rocky, Crowd
Jean Vander Pyl	Wilma
Bea Benaderet	Betty
Don Messick	Arnold, Senior, Professor, Bronto, Bill
John Stephenson	Slate, Doc, Hammerslag

Determined to rise from his job at the gravel pit, Fred attends night school where he is drafted as quarterback of the varsity eleven. Scouted by his own boss, Slate, a Prinstone alumnus, hapless Fred is caught in a day and night grind of work, study, and football practice with halfbacks twice his size. Exhausted by the time of the big game with Shale U., he gives instructions to his teammates on punting the ball. "When I nod my head, you kick it between the goal posts." His teammates take his instructions literally, and both Fred and the ball are propelled through the air to win the game.

THE BEAUTY CONTEST

36

Production No.: P-36
Story: Warren Foster
Recording Date: 4/27/61
Air Date: 12/1/61

Voices:

Alan Reed	Fred, "B" Voice
Mel Blanc	Barney, Dino, Bird
Jean Vander Pyl	Wilma, "A" Girl
Bea Benaderet	Betty, Cookie, "B" Girl
John Stephenson	Guard, King, Guy, Fellow, Boss, Charlie, "C" Voice
Leo de Lyon	Man, Lucky, "A" Voice, John Charles

As loyal members of the Water Buffalo lodge, Fred and Barney are named judges of the beauty contest. Their troubles—trying to keep the event a secret from their wives—mount as Fred is pressured by Mr. Slate to vote for his daughter and Barney is coerced by Big Louie ("Mr. Rackets himself") to vote for his girlfriend, Cookie. Suspicious, Wilma and Betty follow the boys to the Lodge and enter the contest. Under the worst threat of coercion yet, the boys crown their wives as the queens. A riot ensues among the Water Buffalos as the Flintstones and Rubbles make a break for it.

THE MISSING BUS

37

Production No.: P-37
Story: Larry Markes
Recording Date: 4/24/61
Air Date: 9/29/61

Voices:

Alan Reed	Fred, Kid
Mel Blanc	Barney, Bird,
	Nick, Kid
Jean Vander Pyl	Wilma,
	Mrs. Gabbustone, Kid
Bea Benaderet	Betty, Mrs. Rosin,
	Mrs. Carborundum,
	Woman, Kid
Don Messick	Pebbles, Robby, Alvin,
	1st Photographer,
	Kid, 2nd Driver
Hal Smith	A. A. Carborundum,
	2nd Photographer, Kid
Sandra Gould	Mrs. Gypsum,
	Bruce, Kid
Pattee Chapman	Rosalie,
	Nurse, Kid
John Stephenson	Flugel,
	3rd Photographer,
	Mr. Granite, Kid

Leaving his quarry job, Fred becomes the driver of School Bus No. 9 on the dreaded Bedrock to Red Rock run. A shaken man after his first mission—delivering fifty children to school, with Barney as copilot—Fred stops for a well-deserved coffee break at a diner catering to jittery school bus drivers, and is advised to go right out again before he loses his nerve. On the return trip, minus Barney's assistance, he misdelivers all the kids but manages to get an expectant mother to the hospital in the nick of time. The woman gives birth to triplets, all girls, all of whom she names Fred. With a promotion and pay increase from former boss Mr. Granite (Mr. Slate with another name), Fred Flintstone happily goes back to work at the quarry at a far less stressful position—dynamite truck driver.

SOCIAL CLIMBERS

38

Production No.: P-38
Story: Warren Foster
Recording Date: 5/10/61
Air Date: 11/17/61

Voices:

Alan Reed	Fred, 1st Cop
Mel Blanc	Barney, Rocky,
	2nd Man, 2nd Cop
Jean Vander Pyl	Wilma, Right Dame,
	"C" Woman
Bea Benaderet	Betty, Newsboy,
	Left Dame,
	"B" Woman
Paula Winslowe	Emmy,
	Miss Shadrock,
	Dame
John Stephenson	Butler, Spikie,
	Man, 1st Man,
	3rd Cop
Hal Smith	Mr. Hardrock, Man,
	3rd Man, Ambassador,
	Fireman

Fred and Barney generously forego the annual fireman's ball to attend the uppercrust ambassador's reception to which the girls have wangled invitations. At Betty and Wilma's insistence, they go to Bedrock's charm school to train for the white-tie event. Despite taking classes, once at the ball, the Flintstones and Rubbles don't quite fit in with the stuffy crowd. ("Mr. and Mrs. Rubbish," the butler announces as the Rubbles enter.) But when the boys foil a pair of jewel thieves, they're accepted and the society crowd goes with them to the fireman's ball.

THE HOUSE GUEST

39

Production No.: P-39
Story: Sydney Zelinka
Recording Date: 5/15/61
Air Date: 12/22/61

Voices:

Alan Reed	Fred
Mel Blanc	Barney, Porcupine,
	Plumber,
	Woodpecker
Jean Vander Pyl	Wilma
Bea Benaderet	Betty

While plumbers are busy at the Rubble home, Fred invites Betty and Barney to spend the week with him and Wilma. The wives are dismayed at this prospect, foreseeing a week of Fred and Barney fighting, but they agree nonetheless. It doesn't take long for the girls' prediction to come true. Barney makes Fred sleep on the chair; sleepy Fred puts out Barney instead of the cat; and Barney eats all the pizza—the last straw for Fred. Finally the girls end up in a fight, but when they're caught by the boys, everyone has to laugh.

ALVIN BRICKROCK PRESENTS

40

Production No.: P-40
Story: Larry Markes
Recording Date: 5/21/61
Air Date: 10/6/61

Voices:

Alan Reed	Fred
Mel Blanc	Barney,
	Porcupine, Dog
Jean Vander Pyl	Wilma
Bea Benaderet	Betty
Don Messick	Arnold
Elliott Field	Alvin

When the wife of one of Fred's neighbors suddenly disappears, Fred suspects the husband of foul play. After reading a detective magazine, he decides that mild-mannered Alvin Brickrock (who looks and sounds like Alfred Hitchcock) may actually be Albert Bonehart, wanted as a three-time wife-killer. While the magazine says Bonehart is 5'10" (Brickrock is about 4'10"), both men have "difficulty pronouncing 'good evening.'" This is cause enough for Fred and Barney to sneak into the man's house and investigate. They stumble across a mastodon skeleton and a mummy case, which Barney is convinced contains Agatha Brickrock. When Fred discovers a heavy monogrammed trunk which Brickrock claims is for his wife's body, they think they've cracked the case, but it turns out to contain weights and barbells.

THE PICNIC

41

Production No.: P-41
Story: Jack Raymond
Recording Date: 5/20/61
Air Date: 12/15/61

Voices:

Alan Reed	Fred, 1st Guy, Cheers
Mel Blanc	Barney, Turtle, Official,
	3rd Guy, Cuckoo, Dino,
	Bird, 1st Voice,
	2nd Voice, Alligator
Jean Vander Pyl	Wilma, Cheers
Bea Benaderet	Betty, Rita, Cheers
John Stephenson	Joe, Emcee,
	2nd Guy, Cheers

Coveting the trophy collection of Lodge brother Joe Rockhead, Fred decides to change partners for the annual field day games and dumps Barney for tough guy Joe. After Fred fails in three races, Rockhead discards him, and Fred and Barney team up again. With Barney as passenger in the wheelbarrow race, Fred poops out and they change places. Even though the wheelbarrow self-destructs, the team of Flintstone and Rubble manages to beat Rockhead to the finish line and win first prize.

THE MASQUERADE BALL

42

Production No.: P-42
Story: Jack Raymond
Recording Date: 6/12/61
Air Date: 12/8/61

Voices:

Alan Reed	Fred
Mel Blanc	Barney,
	#1 Bird, Dino
Jean Vander Pyl	Wilma
Bea Benaderet	Betty,
	Mrs. Rockhead
John Stephenson	Rockhead,
	O'Shale
Don Messick	Stoneface, Man

Fred's boss Mr. Rockhead (Mr. Slate with a different name) talks him into buying tickets to a society ball. When Fred learns Rockhead will be wearing a turtle costume, he plans to capitalize on this knowledge by buttering up to his boss. At the ball, Fred, failing to realize that his boss has changed costumes, mistakenly tells Rockhead that his boss is the vice president of the moron section of the Bedrock Knucklehead Club. Then he goes off to woo the wearer of the turtle head, but it's too late; Rockhead has heard everything.

THE X-RAY STORY

43

Production No.: P-43
Story: Warren Foster
Recording Date: 6/15/61
Air Date: 12/29/61

Voices:

Alan Reed	Fred
Mel Blanc	Barney, Cat, Dino,
	Man, Cop, Bird
Jean Vander Pyl	Wilma
Bea Benaderet	Betty, Nurse
John Stephenson	Doctor,
	2nd Doctor

Ailing Dino is taken to the vet, who diagnoses his trouble as a dinopeptic germ, fairly harmless in dinosaurs but extremely dangerous to humans. When a policeman finds Dino's X-rays with Fred's name on them, he consults a doctor. The doctor tells Wilma that poor Fred must be kept awake for seventy-two hours and not told why. She and the Rubbles take him dancing and skating and pour cup after cup of coffee down his throat, but he gets sleepier and sleepier. Finally, in desperation, they tell him about his "disease" to keep him awake. After telling them who the X-rays really belong to, Fred promptly falls asleep.

THE ENTERTAINER

44

Production No.: P-44
Story: Arthur Phillips
Recording Date: 6/19/61
Air Date: 1/19/62

Voices:

Alan Reed	Fred
Mel Blanc	Barney, Waiter,
	Doorman, Cuckoo
Jean Vander Pyl	Wilma
Bea Benaderet	Betty, Mrs. Slate
John Stephenson	Slate
Paula Winslow	Greta

Mr. Slate gives Fred an expense account so he can court an important lady buyer. Although he feels guilty about taking "another woman" out to dinner, Wilma's out of town so he agrees. When Wilma returns early, she and the Rubbles go out to dinner at the Copa Cave, where they run into her old friend, Greta Gravel and her date, "Freddie." Poor Fred tries to hide under the table and then crawls out the door, but Wilma invites Greta home. Fred refuses to get out of bed, claiming reversable mumps, but Greta ends up spilling the beans about her date. Heartbroken, Wilma packs a suitcase and prepares to leave until Greta lectures her on how lucky she is to have a husband like Fred.

THE GAMBLER

45

Production No.: P-45
Story: Warren Foster
Recording Date: 6/20/61
Air Date: 1/5/62

Voices:

Alan Reed	Fred
Mel Blanc	Barney
Jean Vander Pyl	Wilma
Bea Benaderet	Betty
Don Messick	Arnold, Voice
John Stephenson	Doctor,
	Announcer, Voice
Alan Dinehart	Voice

Leafing through old picture albums with Betty reminds Wilma of the early days of her marriage when Fred had a gambling problem. Although he has remained cured since undergoing psychiatric consultation, Fred has a relapse and is soon wagering his newspaper bill with Arnold in a fierce game of marbles. Before long, the Flintstones' furniture begins disappearing as Fred's debts increase. Then Barney makes a bet and loses his TV set to Fred, who already lost his own to Arnold. After Arnold's boys club ends up with the entire Flintstone living room suite, Wilma borrows money from Betty—who gets it from Barney's bowling ball stash—to buy new furniture.

WILMA'S VANISHING MONEY

46

Production No.: P-46
Story: Harvey Bullock
Recording Date: 7/5/61
Air Date: 1/26/62

Voices:

Alan Reed	Fred
Mel Blanc	Barney, Policeman
Jean Vander Pyl	Wilma
Bea Benaderet	Betty
Herschel Bernardi	Silky
Don Messick	Arnold
Frank Nelson	Clerk

Looking for a hairpin to fix the toaster, Fred discovers Wilma's secret cash hidden in a drawer. He decides to teach her a lesson by spending the money on a new bowling ball, not realizing that she's been saving up to buy him a new ball for his birthday. Wilma thinks the money's been stolen. and refuses to believe Fred when she catches him replacing it. She thinks he's sweetly giving her his own money and refuses to accept it. In desperation, Fred pays a burglar to put the money back in the drawer. Arnold, playing detective, catches the burglar-for-hire in the act and ties him up. When Wilma arrives on the scene, she feels so sorry for the man that she ends up giving him all the money.

A STAR IS ALMOST BORN

47

Production No.: P-47
Story: Arthur Phillips
Recording Date: 7/10/61
Air Date: 1/12/62

Voices:

Alan Reed	Fred
Mel Blanc	Barney
Jean Vander Pyl	Wilma
Bea Benaderet	Betty
John Stephenson	2nd Man,
	Cowboy,
	Professor, Slate
Frank Nelson	Rockbind
Hal Smith	Soda Jerk, Referee,
	Announcer

Stopping for a snack at a new drugstore, Wilma is in the right place at the right time and is "discovered" by famous TV producer Norman Rockbind. When Fred learns that she's scheduled for a rehearsal, he borrows money from Barney to give her deportment lessons and quits his job to manage her career. But when Wilma's big break turns out to be a commercial advertising hand cream, Fred yanks her out of the studio. Betty takes her place and nets $200—exactly the amount it cost to pay for Wilma's lessons.

OPERATION BARNEY

48

Production No.: P-48
Story: Tony Benedict
Recording Date: 8/16/61
Air Date: 2/16/62

Voices:

Alan Reed	Fred
Mel Blanc	Barney, Dino, Bird
Jean Vander Pyl	Wilma,
	2nd Nurse
Bea Benaderet	Betty,
	1st Nurse
John Stephenson	Voice, Intern,
	German Doctor
Paula Winslow	3rd Nurse
Herschel Bernardi	1st Doctor

En route to work with Barney, Fred makes an executive decision—they'll call in sick so they can take in a ball game. Fred's deathbed routine gets him safely out for the day, but nervous Barney flubs his lines and is ordered to report to the company nurse—a shrew with an eye for layabouts—for a health check. Fred tries to help by boosting Barney's temperature to three hundred degrees with a cigarette lighter. Poor Barney is rushed to the hospital and the surgeons prepare to operate. To save his friend, Fred doubles as a doctor, applies a pipe wrench to Barney's nose, gives it a couple of good twists, pronounces his patient cured, and rolls him out of the hospital at a run. Back at home, they learn that Barney's boss, Mr. Pebbles, was going to give him tickets to the ball game, but because of his "illness," gave them to someone else.

IMPRACTICAL JOKER

49

Production No.: P-49
Story: Warren Foster
Recording Date: 7/24/61
Air Date: 2/9/62

Voices:

Alan Reed	Fred
Mel Blanc	Barney
Jean Vander Pyl	Wilma
Bea Benaderet	Betty
Don Messick	Man, Joe (Diner)
John Stephenson	Joe Rockhead

Fred's been driving Barney crazy with his practical jokes, so Barney decides to give him a taste of his own medicine. Using as bait his winnings from the Sudsy-Wudsy jingle contest—five crisp, new, hundred-dollar bills, Barney sets up a scam with himself as a home basement counterfeiter. Fred falls for the scheme and, in a panic, accompanies Barney all over town, paying for everything his bosom buddy tries to buy. The tables turn when the girls take over the joke and have a "gangster" hold up the boys and take them at gunpoint to Barney's surprise birthday party.

FEUDIN' AND FUSSIN'

50

Production No.: P-50
Story: Arthur Phillips
Recording Date: 7/31/61
Air Date: 2/2/62

Voices:

Alan Reed	Fred
Mel Blanc	Barney, Dino, Elephant
Jean Vander Pyl	Wilma
Bea Benaderet	Betty
John Stephenson	Sam
Hal Smith	Tex

Feuding begins when Fred insults Barney one time too many after Barney's chip shot smacks Fred in the noggin during a pre-golf tournament nap. "I always insult Barney. He's my best friend," Fred tells Wilma defensively. Although his feelings are hurt, good-natured Barney wants to call off the feud, but Betty won't let him, insisting that Fred apologize first. Things go from bad to worse and soon the Rubbles are selling their house. Fred foils the sale by telling the buyer a freeway is going to be built right through the house. The buyer reneges and Fred finally apologizes to his pal.

THE HAPPY HOUSEHOLD

51

Production No.: P-51
Story: Warren Foster
Recording Date: 8/21/61
Air Date: 2/23/62

Voices:

Alan Reed	Fred
Mel Blanc	Barney, Mother
Jean Vander Pyl	Wilma, Women
Bea Benaderet	Betty, Women
John Stephenson	Chef, Agent, Rockbound
Paul Frees	Announcer, Rockenschpeel, Bedrock

After a battle over the household budget with Fred, Wilma applies for an office job at the Bedrock Radio & Television Corporation. Instead, she gets a gig as the star of "The Happy Housewife Show," sponsored by Rockenschpeel Fine Foods. Singing merrily about keeping "your hubby happy," she parades past the cameras every dinner hour bearing platters laden with tempting treats. Fred is miserable, as are the Rubbles, who have naively volunteered to feed him for the thirty-nine weeks of Wilma's contract. All seems lost until the head of a rival TV network threatens to star Fred in a new series, "The Neglected Husband," and Wilma's show is dropped.

THIS IS YOUR LIFESAVER

52

Production No.: P-52
Story: Larry Markes
Recording Date: 9/1/61
Air Date: 3/9/62

Voices:

Alan Reed	Fred
Mel Blanc	Barney, Bird, Whistle
Jean Vander Pyl	Wilma
Bea Benaderet	Betty
John Stephenson	Mr. Slate
Walker Edmiston	Monty

Crossing the George Washingstone Bridge, Fred and Barney come upon a stranger with a boulder tied to his neck. When he asks them to witness his will before he takes his life, Fred rescues the penniless J. Montague Gypsum and takes him home. "Monty" takes over Fred's bed, his robe, his razor, and his kitchen. Fred decides that the only way to get rid of him is to make Monty save his life, thus evening the score. With Barney's help, Fred plots to roll a boulder down a hill at the gravel pit, which Monty, hopefully, will stop. Instead, Monty, while running from the boulder, gets squashed. Mr. Slate believes he saved Fred and makes Monty a foreman.

FRED STRIKES OUT

53

Production No.: P-53
Story: Joanna Lee
Recording Date: 9/7/61
Air Date: 3/2/62

Voices:

Alan Reed	Fred
Mel Blanc	Barney, Dino, Reporter
Jean Vander Pyl	Wilma
Bea Benaderet	Betty

Poor Fred is rated as an inconsiderate spouse by Wilma's magazine quiz on the eighth anniversary of the night he proposed marriage, which of course he forgot. Agreeing to celebrate with a movie date at the drive-in, Fred finds himself in a quandary—the championship bowling tournament is being held at the Bedrock Bowl on the same night. Since the alley is only half a block from the drive-in, he figures he can be in two places at once—almost. But when his thumb gets caught in the bowling ball, he's hard pressed to hide his machinations. And when Barney's attempts to free him have Fred flying through the house as a human cannon ball, he fails completely. Besides, Wilma has already seen his winning photo in the paper. But she's not angry; she gave herself the same quiz and received a lower score than Fred.

THE ROCK VEGAS CAPER

54

Production No.: P-54
Story: Warren Foster
Recording Date: 9/21/61
Air Date: 3/30/62

Voices:

Alan Reed	Fred
Mel Blanc	Barney, Son, Dino
Jean Vander Pyl	Wilma, 2nd Girl
Bea Benaderet	Betty, Lady, Girl
Don Messick	Sherman, Charney
John Stephenson	Mike, Captain, Flirt, Announcer

Dining with Barney at the new Bedrock Rockomat, Fred runs into his old pal Sherman Cobblehead, owner of the Golden Cactus Hotel in Rock Vegas. Cobblehead's casual promise that he will "take care of" Fred should he ever visit leads Fred to pack up his wife, car and neighbors, and head on out. Once in Vegas, Fred loses all their money gambling. Sherman offers to put them "up on the house," but Fred refuses, so Cobblehead says they can reimburse him by helping out. Wilma takes a turn as a cigarette girl, Betty takes pictures of the guests, Barney waits tables, and Fred officiates as maitre d' of the Cactus Room. Barney and Betty also do a snappy stage revue singing "When You're Smiling," and playing the piano. When the vacation is over, everyone agrees it was the best one they've ever had.

THE MAILMAN COMETH

55

Production No.: P-55
Story: Arthur Phillips
Recording Date: 9/25/61
Air Date: 3/23/62

Voices:

Alan Reed	Fred
Mel Blanc	Barney, Brontosaurus, Bird
Jean Vander Pyl	Wilma
Bea Benaderet	Betty, Secretary
John Stephenson	Mailman, 2nd Mailman
Herb Vigran	Cop, Man

Fred, the only employee who hasn't received notice of his annual raise, is fuming. After he writes a nasty letter to his boss and mails it, Mr. Slate comes calling to apologize; Fred has been the victim of a bookkeeping error. Afraid to show up for work and afraid to tell his wife what he's done, Fred lays low by playing sick. His letter is returned to the house for postage and Wilma, trying not to disturb him, pays it and sends it back to Mr. Slate. When Fred finally confesses, Wilma intercepts the letter in the boss's office, "accidentally" breaks his glasses, and "reads" the letter to him. In her version, Fred tells Slate what a wonderful boss he is. Delighted, Slate decides to keep the letter, so Wilma "accidentally" breaks it as well.

TROUBLE-IN-LAW

56

Production No.: P-56
Story: Joanna Lee
Recording Date: 11/6/61
Air Date: 3/16/62

Voices:

Alan Reed	Fred
Mel Blanc	Barney, Bird, Fish, Engineer, 2nd Man
Jean Vander Pyl	Wilma
Bea Benaderet	Betty, Dame
Verna Felton	Mrs. Slaghoople
John Stephenson	1st Man, Joe, Andre, Barker
Hal Smith	Muchrocks

Fred is a desperate man when his mother-in-law arrives for a visit and surprises him with the news that she's sold her home. When he meets Melville J. Muchrocks, a wealthy rancher from Gold Nugget, Texas, he introduces him to "Mama." It's love at first sight, but when Wilma overhears that a con man posing as a wealthy Texan is preying on women in town, Fred and Barney are called upon to save the day. They kidnap Muchrocks from an intimate dinner with Mrs. Slaghoople and throw him on an outbound train. Mama is heartbroken and begins making Fred's life miserable. When she gets a check from the oil well her erstwhile suitor had her invest in, she packs her bags and sets off to find him and rope him in. Overjoyed, Fred works so hard picking up her luggage that he hurts his back, and Mrs. Slaghoople decides to stay and nurse him back to health.

DIVIDED WE SAIL

57

Production No.: P-57
Story: Larry Markes
Recording Date: 12/13/61
Air Date: 4/6/62

Voices:

Alan Reed — Fred
Mel Blanc — Barney, Turtle, Driver, Monster
Jean Vander Pyl — Wilma
Bea Benaderet — Betty, Agatha
John Stephenson — Emery, Announcer, Sludge
Hal Smith — Will, Cop

Fred receives a ticket to be a contestant on the TV game show, "The Prize Is Priced," but when he gets cold feet, Barney goes on instead and promptly wins a houseboat. An argument ensues over who it belongs to, the Flintstones or the Rubbles. Deciding to share ownership, the two couples christen the little boat the Nau-Sea, and take it out for a cruise. In the harbor, a sea monster swallows the Nau-Sea's anchor and pulls its far from shore, where it hits a rock and begins to sink. The girls hop into a life raft, but Fred and Barney, arguing over who is the captain, go down with the ship.

KLEPTOMANIA CAPER

58

Production No.: P-58
Story: Joanna Lee
Recording Date: 1/3/62
Air Date: 4/13/62

Voices:

Alan Reed — Fred
Mel Blanc — Barney, Rockowski, Voice
Jean Vander Pyl — Wilma, Salesgirl
Bea Benaderet — Betty, Woman
Herb Vigran — Cop
Herschel Bernardi — Detective
John Stephenson — Announcer, Doctor

Planning a trip to the Ladies Auxiliary rummage sale, Wilma cleans all of Fred's old junk out of the hall closet. When Fred discovers his beloved things are missing, he calls the police. Meanwhile, Wilma and Betty load the stuff into Barney's car, and when the missing items are discovered in it, the investigating cop tells Fred his bosom buddy is a kleptomaniac. Later, Betty asks Barney to pick up some things at the Bedrock Department Store and Fred goes along to keep an eye on him. The store detective thinks Barney is a thief, and in the resultant confusion, both Fred and Barney end up in jail. The girls bail them out, and Wilma suffers an attack of conscience and tries to recoup Fred's things—but she gets mixed up and grabs Joe Rockhead's instead.

LATIN LOVER

59

Production No.: P-59
Story: Harvey Bullock
Recording Date: 1/5/62
Air Date: 4/20/62

Voices:

Alan Reed — Fred
Mel Blanc — Barney, 2nd Bird, Penguin, Bird, Dino
Jean Vander Pyl — Wilma
Bea Benaderet — Betty
Paula Winslow — Woman's Voice, Saleslady, Mrs. Slate
Jerry Mann — Roberto, Policeman
John Stephenson — Announcer, Mr. Slate, Airport Announcer

After seeing Roberto Rockelini on TV, Wilma sets out to re-create Fred into a reasonable facsimile. Soon he's wearing an ascot and moustache and is phrase-dropping in Italian. But when Dino knocks over a pretty cosmetics saleslady and she falls into Fred's arms, Wilma and Betty determine that the Fred has a little too much sex appeal. Wilma tries to change him back into rumpled Fred, but he resists. Then, when Mr. Slate asks Fred to take his wife to the airport, Wilma thinks he's running off with another woman. Following them, she throws herself at her husband's feet in front of the Slates. Fred convinces her she's been mistaken about his appeal to the ladies, decides he's not the Latin-lover type anyway, and reverts to his old self.

TAKE ME OUT TO THE BALL GAME

60

Production No.: P-60
Story: Larry Markes
Recording Date: 1/15/62
Air Date: 4/27/62

Voices:

Alan Reed — Fred
Mel Blanc — Barney, Bird, Dino, Stegosaurus
Jean Vander Pyl — Wilma, Clarence, Melvin, Norman, Sandy
Bea Benaderet — Betty, Slugger
Hal Smith — Scout, Pa, Red
John Stephenson — Slate, Arnold's Father, Father, Coach
Don Messick — Arnold, Kid #2

Fred accompanies Peewee League baseball coach Barney to a practice session before the big game between his team, the Bedrock Giants, and their arch rivals, the Grittsburg Pyrites. The players—including Arnold and Mr. Slate's son Eugene—choose Fred to umpire. At the game, Fred calls the winning play in the Pyrites' favor and is set upon by the Giants' angry fathers. The Giants apologize for their parents' behavior and with Fred as their spokesman, donate all their equipment to the dads so they can form their own team and learn fair play.

160

FRED'S NEW BOSS

61

Production No.: P-61
Story: Warren Foster
Recording Date: 2/1/62
Air Date: 9/21/62

Voices:

Alan Reed	Fred
Mel Blanc	Barney, Bird, Pelican,
	Dinosaur, Dino
Jean Vander Pyl	Wilma, Alice
Bea Benaderet	Betty, Lady Spieler
John Stephenson	Mediator, Pierre,
	Mr. Slate, Butler
Herb Vigran	Cop, Man

When Barney gets laid off from work, Fred volunteers to get him a job at the gravel pit. Initially rejecting Barney, Slate relents when he discovers he's Barney's uncle, and hires him on as executive vice president in charge of production. It's an arrangement that pleases no one. Fred and Wilma are resentful of Barney's new position and the Rubbles are unhappy socializing with the other executives (at a chess tournament Barney asks if anyone wants to shoot pool). As a result, Barney quits his job—Betty doesn't want him working for relatives—and everyone makes up.

DINO GOES HOLLYROCK

62

Production No.: P-62
Story: Harvey Bullock
Recording Date: 1/30/62
Air Date: 9/14/62

Voices:

Alan Reed	Fred
Mel Blanc	Barney, Dino,
	Bird, Checker,
	Monkey, Sheep
Jean Vander Pyl	Wilma, Belle,
	Sassie
Bea Benaderet	Betty, Girl
John Stephenson	Director,
	Announcer
Herschel Bernardi	Villain, Agent
Hal Smith	Sportscaster,
	Champ
Don Messick	Junior

Dino is ousted from Fred's favor—and the Flintstone home—for his annoying devotion to his favorite TV show, "The Adventures of Sassie." Then Fred learns the show is holding a search for dinosaurs with acting talent, and he begins training Dino for stardom, using Barney as a model. Dino is a sensation at his audition, but when he learns that the studio plans to give him contact lenses, cap his teeth, crop his tail, and make him go out every night with Sassie—who is much less than she seems to be—he runs home to Fred.

THE TWITCH

63

Production No.: P-63
Story: Joanna Lee
Recording Date: 2/14/62
Air Date: 10/12/62

Voices:

Alan Reed	Fred
Mel Blanc	Barney, Dino,
	Bird, Peeler
Jean Vander Pyl	Wilma
Bea Benaderet	Betty
Hal Smith	Rock
John Stephenson	Sam,
	Announcer, Emcee
Ginny Tyler	Blonde

Wilma is in a dither over finding an act for her ladies club benefit show until Fred promises he'll line one up. His old buddy, talent agent Sam Stone, fails him, and Fred sees country-western singing sensation Rock Roll performing his hit song, "The Twitch," on TV. Fred first tells Wilma he's signed Rock, and then begs the man to do the show. Rock agrees, but come showtime he can't perform—an allergic reaction to pickled dodo eggs has rendered him temporarily mute. He hands his wig, costume, and guitar to Fred, who lip syncs the song on stage to great acclaim. Afterwards, Fred quits his job to pursue a singing career.

INVISIBLE BARNEY

64

Production No.: P-64
Story: Teleplay by
Warren Foster
Recording Date: 3/24/62
Air Date: 9/28/62

Voices:

Alan Reed	Fred
Mel Blanc	Barney, Seal, Parrot,
	Bird, Dino
Jean Vander Pyl	Wilma
Bea Benaderet	Betty, Nurse
John Stephenson	1st Cop,
	Blowhard
Hal Smith	Announcer,
	2nd Cop
Howard McNear	Doctor

When Fred offers Barney a swig of his experimental soft drink to stop his hiccups, Barney becomes invisible. Fred tries to keep this a secret from the girls, but his strange behavior worries Wilma and she packs him off to see the doctor. The doctor can't cure Barney (who came with Fred), so the friends head for home. On the way, the invisibility wears off, but meanwhile, Dino's drunk the formula and now he's invisible.

BOWLING BALLET

65

Production No.: P-65

Story: Teleplay
by Warren Foster

Recording Date: 4/3/62

Air Date: 10/5/62

Voices:

Alan Reed	Fred, 2nd Rock
Mel Blanc	Barney, Guy, Parrot, Dino
Jean Vander Pyl	Wilma, Girl, Dancer
Bea Benaderet	Betty, Miss Kay, Dancer
John Stephenson	Charlie, 1st Guy, Slate, Announcer, 1st Voice
Hal Smith	2nd Guy, 1st Rock, 2nd Voice, Teammate

Fred loses his sense of timing just before his bowling team's crucial match against the Rockland Rockets. Desperate to regain his form, Fred sees a TV commercial advertising rhythm as "the secret of success in many activities including bowling," and hurries to the Bedrock Dance Studio to sign up as a ballet pupil. Finding him with a bevy of ballerinas, Wilma makes him quit, but when he bowls ballet style and wins the match, she forgives him.

BABY BARNEY

66

Production No.: P-66

Story: Warren Foster

Recording Date: 5/23/62

Air Date: 11/9/62

Voices:

Alan Reed	Fred, Man
Mel Blanc	Barney, Bird, Doll, Baby, Charlie, Cop, Sergeant
Jean Vander Pyl	Wilma, Lady
Bea Benaderet	Betty, 2nd Lady, Old Maid
Hal Smith	Boy, Clerk, Orville, Tex

Fred worries he'll be disinherited when his rich Uncle Tex arrives and learns the truth—the namesake that Fred so glowingly described in his letters to his uncle doesn't exist. Becoming desperate when he's unable to borrow a "loaner" baby for a few days, Fred convinces a reluctant Barney to play little Tex. While portraying the infant, Barney antagonizes Fred in every available manner until he gets fed up himself and drives off. Uncle Tex gives chase in his impossibly long limo; Fred, Wilma, and Betty chase Tex; and the police chase all of them. Once at the police station, the truth comes out, but Uncle Tex decides Fred can have his inheritance anyway.

THE BUFFALO CONVENTION

67

Production No.: P-67

Story: Warren Foster

Recording Date: 4/12/62

Air Date: 10/26/62

Voices:

Alan Reed	Fred, Voice
Mel Blanc	Barney, Dino, Elephant, Doozey, Monkey
Jean Vander Pyl	Wilma, 1st Gal, 3rd Gal
Bea Benaderet	Betty, Mrs. Stonewall, 2nd Gal
John Stephenson	Mailman, Doc, Poobah, Driver
Hal Smith	Peddler, Emcee, Guard

Promising each of the Water Buffalos "a three day rest away from home," the Grand Poobah sends Dr. Ben Casement—in actuality a plumber—out to make house calls and diagnose dipsy-doodle-itis. The cure: three days of solitude at Frantic City, where the Lodge just happens to be having its convention. When Wilma's talking dodo bird Doozey overhears the ruse and spills the beans, Wilma, Betty, and a busload of angry Lodge wives descend upon the convention. Replacing the girls who had been hired, the wives jump out of a cake onstage. The boys escape to the boardwalk, but once again Doozey gives away their whereabouts. The fiasco ends underwater, with Fred and Barney holding onto strands of seaweed and their noses, and Doozey swimming by, still repeating everything they say.

HERE'S SNOW IN YOUR EYES

68

Production No.: P-68

Story: Joanna Lee

Recording Date: 5/2/62

Air Date: 10/19/62

Voices:

Alan Reed	Fred
Mel Blanc	Barney, Animal, 3rd Reporter, Porcupine
Jean Vander Pyl	Wilma, Maid
Bea Benaderet	Betty, Brunette
John Stephenson	TV Announcer, Butler, Cop, 2nd Reporter
Doug Young	Photographer, Chip Marble, 1st Reporter, Clerk

When Fred and Barney attend a Lodge convention at the Stone Mountain Ski Resort without their wives, Wilma and Betty don disguises and follow them. The girls are mistaken for beauty contestants, but after having their pictures taken in swimsuits on the ice, they decide that the glamorous life is not for them. Meanwhile, jewel thieves posing as maid and butler pass a stolen diamond to Barney, believing him to be their contact. When the thieves realize they've passed the jewel to the wrong man, the chase is on. Barney and Fred trick them into skiing off a cliff. The crooks are arrested, and the boys are declared heroes.

THE LITTLE STRANGER

 69

Production No.: P-69
Story: Herb Finn
Recording Date: 5/9/62
Air Date: 11/2/62

Voices:

Alan Reed	Fred
Mel Blanc	Barney, Bird, Dino, Guy, Turtle, Hector
Jean Vander Pyl	Wilma
Bea Benaderet	Betty, Woman
Don Messick	Arnold, Doctor
Verna Felton	Mother

Fred gets up on the wrong side of bed, and before the day is over, his bad temper is pinpointed at Arnold, the newspaper-delivery boy. Meanwhile, Wilma invites Arnold to spend two weeks with them while his parents are out of town. Afraid to tell Fred until the last possible moment, she keeps the news to herself, but when Fred overhears that she's expecting "a little stranger," he decides Wilma's pregnant. His bad mood evaporates. He fixes her breakfast in bed and even invites her mother, Mrs. Slaghoople, to stay—but only because baby nurses are too expensive. Fred only learns the truth when the little stranger, Arnold, arrives on the doorstep, at the same time as Mrs. Slaghoople.

LADIES DAY

 70

Production No.: P-70
Story: Harvey Bullock
Recording Date: 5/25/62
Air Date: 11/23/62

Voices:

Alan Reed	Fred
Mel Blanc	Barney, Rocko, Bronto, Dino, Seapy
Jean Vander Pyl	Wilma, Fat Woman
Bea Benaderet	Betty, 2nd Woman
John Stephenson	Charlie, Mr. Slate, Ticket Taker, Sarge, 1st Man, 2nd Fan
Don Messick	Skinny, Bellhop, Cop, Ump, Catcher, 1st Fan

Ladies Day at the ballpark—women get in for free—finds Fred, in lipstick and a rummage sale dress, escorted by Barney. When Betty discovers lipstick on her husband's handkerchief, the wives go after their husbands. And the police are after Fred and Barney as well—Barney's been insulting fat ladies under the impression that they're Fred. Worse yet, Mr. Slate and a client are also at the ballpark. The client initially is attracted to "Fredericka," but soon dumps him for Wilma. Jealous Fred throws the man out of the clubhouse, then has Barney wear the dress to sneak past the police. When Barney is defrocked going through the turnstile at the park exit, the chase resumes.

HAWAIIAN ESCAPADE

 71

Production No.: P-71
Story: Joanna Lee
Recording Date: 6/21/62
Air Date: 11/16/62

Voices:

Alan Reed	Fred
Mel Blanc	Barney, Bird, Lizard, Beast
Jean Vander Pyl	Wilma, Stewardess
Bea Benaderet	Betty
John Stephenson	Larry Lava, Goldrock, Joe
Don Messick	C. W. Crater, TV Announcer, Stoneheart, Boy

Tempted by the chance to meet their TV idol, Larry Lava of "Hawaiian Spy," Wilma and Betty enter a contest. When they win, it's off to Rockiki Beach where Fred gets a one-line part in the show. As usual, Flintstone becomes an overbearing "star," and to get rid of him, the producers make him a stuntman. When it's time to shoot his big scene, in which he must fight a dinosaur, Fred runs away and Wilma punches the big beast in the nose. Back at home, Wilma receives a call from the producers. They offer to build a show around her, but she refuses, saying she's a star in her own right as Mrs. Fred Flintstone.

NUTHIN' BUT THE TOOTH

 **72**

Production No.: P-72
Story: Tony Benedict
Recording Date: 6/29/62
Air Date: 11/30/62

Voices:

Alan Reed	Fred
Mel Blanc	Barney, Dino, Parrot, Hector, 2nd Soldier, Bird, Army Pilot, Man, 2nd Bird
Jean Vander Pyl	Wilma, Nurse, Woman
Bea Benaderet	Betty, Woman
Don Messick	Kid, Co-Pilot
Howard Morris	Doctor, Boy, Pilot, 1st Soldier, Sergeant, Cop, 1st Bird

Barney's moans over a late night toothache wake the Flintstones, and Fred promises to drive his buddy to the dentist in the morning. But when daylight dawns, Fred decides to pull the tooth himself, and spend Barney's money on the fights. He ties the tooth to his moving car, but when that only gains him a conk in the head, he takes Barney to Smiley Molar, the dinosaur dentist. Smiley administers too much gas—rendering Barney airborne—so Fred fashions a swing, hangs it from his buddy, and they float above the outdoor fight arena, and watch the action for free.

HIGH SCHOOL FRED

73

Production No.: P-73

Story: Warren Foster

Recording Date: 7/5/62

Air Date: 12/7/62

Voices:

Alan Reed	Fred
Mel Blanc	Barney, Dinosaur, Dino, Boy #2, Bird, Elephant
Jean Vander Pyl	Wilma, Small Girl, Teacher
Bea Benaderet	Betty, Secretary
John Stephenson	Charlie, Mr. Slate, Principal, Announcer
Howard Morris	Mr. Rockhard, Cat, Boy #1, Boy #3, Coach, Charles

An efficiency expert recommends that Fred be fired because he didn't finish high school. But instead of firing Fred, Mr. Slate sends him back to Bedrock High. Fitting right in with the kids, Fred becomes a basketball champ, breaks track records, and hangs out at the malt shop, consuming forty-nine malts and ten brontoburgers in one sitting. No wonder he comes home ill and exhausted every night and collapses into bed. His final school coup, however, does not involve food—he leads the team to a winning football game at the Rock Bowl.

DIAL S FOR SUSPICION

74

Production No.: P-74

Story: Herb Finn

Recording Date: 7/9/62

Air Date: 12/14/62

Voices:

Alan Reed	Fred
Mel Blanc	Barney, Elephant, Dino, Turtle, Pencil Bird
Jean Vander Pyl	Wilma
Bea Benaderet	Betty
Howard Morris	Monkey, Letter Opening Bird, Rodney Whetstone, 2nd Turtle, Dr. Pilldown, 1st Guy in Crowd
John Stephenson	Mailman, Man, Hailstone, Ringmaster, 2nd Guy in Crowd

Fred is accepted as Conrad Hailstone's aide at the exclusive Stone Valley Inn, contingent upon passing a physical. At the same time, he agrees to Wilma's request that he take out life insurance. His suspicions are aroused, however, when he finds her reading a book about doing away with a husband, and they are nearly confirmed when she volunteers him as the object of the knife-throwing act at the circus. Confusing the insurance physical—which he doesn't want to pass—with the Hailstone physical, Fred gets ready for the exam. With Barney as his nurse, he sits in a wheelchair, places an alarm clock in his chest to substitute for his ticker, and borrows a dummy arm from the tailor to make it appear that he has no pulse. Needless to say, he flunks the exam—and loses out on his new job.

FLASH GUN FREDDIE

75

Production No.: P-75

Story: Jack Raymond

Recording Date: 7/16/62

Air Date: 12/21/62

Voices:

Alan Reed	Fred
Mel Blanc	Barney, Elephant, Bird, Baby, Dino, Manager, Baby Birds
Jean Vander Pyl	Wilma, Martha Millrocks, Pterodactyl Mother
Bea Benaderet	Betty
Howard Morris	Clerk, Kid, Porcupine, Reporter, 2nd Hood
John Stephenson	Harvey Millrocks, Mailman, Editor, 1st Hood, Man

Fred gets carried away by the flashy possibilites inherent in a photography career. Borrowing Barney's money, he buys a Polarock camera and the two go into business. They begin with baby pictures, and Fred gets socked in the eye with a tiny fist. They photograph men at work, and Fred gets punched by an errant construction worker. They take nature shots, and Barney is kidnapped by an angry pterodactyl, who drops him on Fred. Finally, the pair sell a photo to the Bedrock Gazette, and thinking they've made it, rush out and purchase every piece of photography equipment on the market—using the Rubbles' money. When Betty says she's going to make a withdrawal at the bank, Fred and Barney beat her there and try to borrow on their equipment so Betty won't discover that the account is now empty. They're turned down, but on the way out they snap a shot of a couple of bank robbers, sell the photo to the paper, and return the Rubbles' money in time.

THE KISSING BURGLAR

76

Production No.: P-76

Story: Teleplay by Joanna Lee

Recording Dates: 7/27/62 and 8/10/62

Air Date: 1/4/63

Voices:

Alan Reed	Fred
Mel Blanc	Barney, Porcupine, Punchy, 2nd Cop
Jean Vander Pyl	Wilma, Gladys
Bea Benaderet	Betty, Wife
Howard Morris	Burglar, Henry, 1st Cop

There's a burglar on the loose in Bedrock and Wilma is charmed by his method—a rose and a kiss for the lady of the house. Fred is miffed when Wilma claims she has no valuables a burglar would want except for her Siberian Tibbar (rabbit spelled backward) coat. Fred decides to teach his wife a lesson by impersonating the Lothario, but while he's en route, the real burglar shows up. When Fred arrives in his yard, dressed in his mask and top hat, he's set upon by the burglar's wife, who—thinking Fred is the real crook—is furious because her husband is kissing all the ladies. Fred finally gets away from her and enters his house to discover the Kissing Burglar and Wilma enacting a scene to make him jealous. The police show up and arrest Fred, but the burglar—a true gentleman—confesses.

THE BIRTHDAY PARTY

 77

Production No.: P-77
Story: Joanna Lee
Recording Date: 8/10/62
Air Date: 4/5/63

Voices:

Alan Reed	Fred
Mel Blanc	Barney, Alligator, Dino, Duck, Bird, Dog, Dinosaur
Jean Vander Pyl	Wilma, Mrs. Slate, Hester
Bea Benaderet	Betty, Mrs. Slag, Esther
Howard Morris	Bird, Animal, 2nd Card Player, Rockhead, Slag
John Stephenson	1st Card Player, Slate
Doug Young	Foreman, Dealer

Wilma, planning a big surprise party for Fred at the Rubbles' house, assigns Barney to occupy him elsewhere. When party time arrives the boys are missing. They're in the steam room at the gym, asleep. When Barney awakens he puts his snoozing pal in the car, which promptly rolls away. After the car, which finally stops at an automobile dealership, is bought and sold—with Fred still asleep inside— Barney finally brings him home. But while Barney runs into the house, Fred accepts an invitation to play bridge with the new neighbors, and misses the party anyway.

WILMA, THE MAID

 78

Production No.: P-78
Story: Harvey Bullock/ R. Saffian
Recording Date: 8/13/62
Air Date: 1/11/63

Voices:

Alan Reed	Fred
Mel Blanc	Barney, Pelican, Porcupine Brush, Henry (Elephant), Bird, Dino, Fur Animal
Jean Vander Pyl	Wilma, Mrs. Vanderock
Bea Benaderet	Betty, Lollabrickida
Howard Morris	Knitting Needle Bird, Ted Stonevan, Filbert (Dinosaur), Tex Bricker, Chisel Bird, Turtle Butler
John Stephenson	Mr. Vanderock, Mr. Slate

Campaigning to get a maid, Wilma tries every angle—including feigned illness—but all to no avail. When she finally resorts to tears, Fred instantly surrenders and earthy Italian Lollobrickida arrives to do the housework. She cooks divinely, setting Fred to singing in the shower, which sets Lollabrickida's teeth on edge. When he says he'll serenade her night and day, she quits, just as Mr. Slate is coming for dinner. Meanwhile, Wilma, doing her friends a favor, is playing the role of a maid to impress the Rubbles' guests, the uppercrust Vanderocks. When Slate discovers Wilma working as a maid, he gives Fred a raise.

THE HERO

 79

Production No.: P-79
Story: Herb Finn
Recording Date: 8/15/62
Air Date: 1/18/63

Voices:

Alan Reed	Fred, Fred's Self
Mel Blanc	Barney, Poobah, Porcupine, Dino, Turtle
Jean Vander Pyl	Wilma, Baby
Bea Benaderet	Betty, Mother
Howard Morris	Quartz, Member #2, Member #4, Ticket Taker, Reporter, #1 Man, Jimmy (Mayor)
Don Messick	Member #1, Member #3, Cop, Stonewall, #2 Man, Arnold

Soaring aloft on a bunch of balloons, Barney rescues a baby from a runaway buggy atop a rollercoaster track, but Fred, who's holding the child when the mother arrives, is proclaimed the hero. When Fred's picture appears in the paper, Barney goes along with the "true" account, and soon Fred is hobnobbing with the mayor and fishing with the governor. Fred tells Barney he didn't save the baby single-handedly, but modest Barney only says, "If I deserve to be a hero, I'll be a hero." Fred can't live with himself—his conscience in ghostly form makes life miserable by stealing his dinner and sneaking into his bed. He finally confesses, and is elected Grand Imperial Poobah by the Lodge for his courage.

FOXY GRANDMA

 80

Production No.: P-80
Story: Herb Finn
Recording Date: 8/30/62
Air Date: 2/8/63

Voices:

Alan Reed	Fred, 2nd Man
Mel Blanc	Barney, Elephant, Parrot, Sonny, #1 Cop, Bird, #2 Cop
Jean Vander Pyl	Wilma, Miss Keystone, Bertha
Bea Benaderet	Betty, Bubbles
Don Messick	Ziegfried, Teller, Newsboy, Radio Voice, 1st Man
June Foray	Peaches, Granny, Bank Customer Voice
Verna Felton	Mother

Mother-to-be Wilma convinces Fred he needs to hire a housekeeper. He contacts the Bedrock Employment Agency. After a few fiascos, Fred encounters Grandma Dynamite (she's robbed the First, Second and Third National Banks and needs a hideout) and brings her home to housekeep. Fred volunteers to drive her to the market, but they stop at the bank instead. "Wait right here and keep the motor running," she tells him. Fred discovers her true identity when she returns with a fistful of dynamite. She and her huge grandson return to the Flintstone home and hold Fred and Wilma hostage. The couple is saved when Mrs. Slaghoople shows up and tosses the crooks out, but the police arrive and cart her off, believing her to be Grandma Dynamite.

THE SURPRISE

81

Production No.: P-81
Story: Warren Foster
Recording Date: 9/4/62
Air Date: 1/25/63

Voices:

Alan Reed	Fred
Mel Blanc	Barney, Dino, Rocky, 2nd Cop
Jean Vander Pyl	Wilma
Bea Benaderet	Betty, Woman
Don Messick	Baby, Guy, Adlib Voice, Teammate, Sarge, 1st Cop

When Barney is attentive to his visiting baby nephew, Marblehead Sandstone, Fred storms out in a jealous fit. Barney has two tickets to the sold-out ball game, though, so Fred forgives him—until he learns that Barney has given the tickets to Joe Rockhead. That night, Fred makes an unkind remark about babies and Wilma bursts into tears. Holding up a tiny bootie, she tells him that they're going to have a baby. Papa-to-be Fred runs out into the yard in delight, yelling the news to the neighborhood and dancing in the moonlight.

MOTHER-IN-LAW'S VISIT

82

Production No.: P-82
Story: Warren Foster
Recording Date: 9/7/62
Air Date: 2/1/63

Voices:

Alan Reed	Fred
Mel Blanc	Barney, Cop, Dino, Alligator, White Lamb
Jean Vander Pyl	Wilma, Nurse
Bea Benaderet	Betty
Howard Morris	Guard, Announcer, Pilot, Traffic Cop, Black Lamb
Verna Felton	Mother

Fred promises pregnant Wilma that he'll be nice to her mother, Mrs. Slaghoople, when she comes to visit. Picking her up at the airport, he offers a smile and a kiss; she hits him with her handbag. When he's stopped by the police for speeding, he tells them his "wife" is expecting, and delivers Mrs. Slaghoople to the maternity hospital—where he leaves her. Later he takes a job as a cab driver—disguised in a cap and a moustache—to earn money for a baby crib. His first passenger is Mrs. Slaghoople, who is looking for her son-in-law whom she thinks is out carousing. They end up spending the evening together, betting with each other over games of pool and bowling. In a final bet, Fred, the cabbie, bets Mrs. Slaghoople that she will find her son-in law in the library. She, of course, disagrees. Fred races into the reading room, removes his disguise, and lets her find him perusing books on baby care. Mrs. Slaghoople becomes his best pal—until Barney spills the beans about the identity of the "cabbie."

FRED'S NEW JOB

83

Production No.: P-83
Story: Teleplay by Warren Foster
Recording Date: 9/11/62
Air Date: 2/15/63

Voices:

Alan Reed	Fred
Mel Blanc	Barney, Goony Bird, Elephant, Dino, Man, Colonel
Jean Vander Pyl	Wilma, Miss LaRock, Gal Voices
Bea Benaderet	Betty, Gal, Gal Voices
John Stephenson	Fireman, Slate
Howard Morris	Eddie, Clam, Turtle, Manager, Customer

With a baby on the way, Fred is in a stew over how to earn more money, and Barney suggests that he ask Mr. Slate for a raise. Slate, who expected this request from the expectant father, mounts Operation Cringe with his son, who also happens to be a manager at the quarry. In a scene staged for Fred's benefit, Eddie begs his father for a raise and then ends up grateful for a pay cut. Barney and Fred then mount Operation Get You A Raise. Wearing a tuxedo and top hat, Barney offers to take Fred off Slate's hands by offering Fred more money. Slate tells "Mr. Rockafeather" he can have him. Newly unemployed, Fred takes a job as a short-order cook at the Brown Turban Drive-In, but quits when the lunch hour crowd proves too hectic. Meanwhile, back at the quarry, Slate and his son find they can't operate the digger or do any business without Flintstone, so they give him his job back with a raise.

THE BLESSED EVENT (ALSO CALLED DRESS REHEARSAL)

84

Production No.: P-84
Story: Harvey Bullock/ R. Saffian
Recording Date: 9/20/60
Air Date: 2/22/63

Voices:

Alan Reed	Fred
Mel Blanc	Barney, Parrot, Dino, Len
Jean Vander Pyl	Wilma, 3rd Nurse, Pebbles
Bea Benaderet	Betty
Howard Morris	Brick, Bird, Doc, Cuckoo Bird, Dr. Corset, Bosun's Whistle
Don Messick	Dog, Windy, Porcupine, Cat, Cop, Clerk, Man
June Foray	1st Nurse, 2nd Nurse

Aware that Wilma could give birth any day, Fred becomes a nervous wreck while waiting to drive her to the hospital. With Barney acting as a substitute mother, Fred makes a successful test run and arrives proudly back home. When Wilma tells him it's time, he drives off to the hospital—with Barney. Finally Wilma arrives at the hospital, and Barney and Fred anxiously pace the waiting room. Later, gathered around Wilma and the new arrival, Barney remarks that she's "a chip off the block," to which Fred replies, "More like a pebble off the old Flintstone," and the baby is named. When Barney asks the baby if she likes it, she coos "Abba dabba doo."

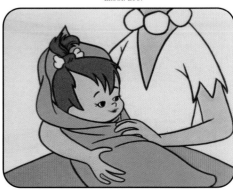

CARRY ON, NURSE FRED

 85

Production No.: P-85
Story by Mike Maltese,
Teleplay by Joanna Lee
Recording Date: 9/27/62
Air Date: 3/1/63

Voices:

Alan Reed	Fred
Mel Blanc	Barney, Dino,
	Rockenheimer
Jean Vander Pyl	Wilma, Pebbles
Bea Benaderet	Betty, Nurse
Doug Young	Cop, Laundry Man

Nurse Frightenshale, hired by Wilma's mother to take care of the house and baby, throws out not only the flowers Barney brings over but Barney and Betty as well. When Fred fires the battle-axe, Wilma informs him that he must do everything while she rests in bed. He sets cheerfully to work but soon becomes exhausted. Leaving Pebbles atop a pile of diapers, he falls asleep. When Fred awakens, Pebbles is gone and he thinks the laundry man must have taken her by mistake. She's with Wilma, but Fred races to the laundry, dives into the washing machine to save the baby, and emerges with a cold. Back home, Nurse Frightenshale, newly rehired, sends Fred to sleep in the garage.

VENTRILOQUIST BARNEY

 86

Production No.: P-86
Story by Mike Maltese,
Teleplay by Herb Finn
Recording Date: 10/2/62
Air Date: 3/8/63

Voices:

Alan Reed	Fred
Mel Blanc	Barney, Bird, Dino,
	Record Player Bird,
	Turtle, Bronto
Jean Vander Pyl	Wilma, Pebbles
Bea Benaderet	Betty
Janet Waldo	Linda, Lady, Hostess
Doug Young	Jerry, Announcer,
	Mauler

Barney uses his ventriloquist abilities to make Fred believe that Pebbles can talk, and then he talks Fred into bringing Pebbles with them to a wrestling match. She crawls into the ring where she is named the champ, and when Wilma and Betty see her on TV, they angrily head out after the baby and the boys. Back at home, Barney throws his voice to make Fred think it's Wilma, yelling at him. When Wilma really arrives, Fred tells her the truth, and, with Barney's help, Pebbles agrees. Both parents promptly faint at the sound of their baby talking.

THE BIG MOVE

 87

Production No.: P-87
Story: Joanna Lee
Recording Date: 10/16/62
Air Date: 3/22/63

Voices:

Alan Reed	Fred
Mel Blanc	Barney, Elephant,
	Dino, Turtle,
	Charlie
Jean Vander Pyl	Wilma, Pebbles,
	2nd Woman
Bea Benaderet	Betty, 1st Woman,
	Mrs. Slate
Howard Morris	Boy,
	Monkey, 1st Man,
	3rd Man, 4th Man,
	Slate, Bird
Doug Young	2nd Man,
	Percy, Egbert

Concerned that Pebbles may pick up Barney's uncouth habits, Fred decides to move his family to a better neighborhood. He signs a lease on a mansion complete with pool, steam room, and tennis court. When the Flintstones discover that their new neighbors are a bunch of snooty freeloaders, and that the new house is too big and quiet, Fred and Wilma decide to go home to their real friends. The Rubbles help them get out of the lease by posing as hillbillies and upsetting the ritzy landlords.

SWEDISH VISITORS

 88

Production No.: P-88
Story by Harvey Bullock/
R. Saffian
Recording Date: 10/23/62
Air Date: 3/29/63

Voices:

Alan Reed	Fred
Mel Blanc	Barney, Teller, Sven,
	Dino, Judge, Gulp
Jean Vander Pyl	Wilma, Pebbles
Bea Benaderet	Betty
Howard Morris	Turtle, Ole,
	Driver, Ranger,
	Voice, Cop
Henry Hoople	Ingmar

Instead of going away on vacation, Fred decides to bank the extra money and relax at home. Wilma goes along with his wishes so she can withdraw the funds and buy herself a fur neckpiece. She's happy with her secret purchase until Fred changes his mind and takes the family camping in their trailer. Trying to recoup the spent money, Wilma rents the house to a Swedish music group while they're gone. The woods are noisy with dynamiting and logging, and, in a special guest appearance, Yogi Bear and Boo-Boo steal the Flintstones' pic-a-nic basket. Fred decides to drive home while Wilma is asleep in the trailer. Upon arriving, Fred discovers the Swedish visitors and he talks Barney into calling the police to have them arrested for disturbing the peace. At the station, the musicians tell the judge how wonderful the Flintstones are and sing a song that they composed in their honor.

DINO DISAPPEARS

89

Production No.: P-89
Story: Joanna Lee
Recording Date: 3/13/63
Air Date: 10/10/63

Voices:

Alan Reed	Fred
Mel Blanc	Barney, Lion, Dino,
	Camera Bird, Officer
Jean Vander Pyl	Wilma, Pebbles,
	Pebbles Doll
Bea Benaderet	Betty
Hal Smith	Pelican, Dinosaur,
	Poodle, 2nd Guy,
	Rocky, Charlie,
	Sergeant
Jerry Hauser	1st Guy, 3rd Guy,
	Owner, Clyde, Turtle

When Fred forgets Dino's anniversary and falsely accuses him of trying to hurt Pebbles, the despondent dinosaur runs away from home. Out searching the streets, Fred and Barney come across a six-foot, purple dinosaur with spots chained in a yard. Fred assumes it must be Dino, but its owner chases him away, so he and Barney come back and steal the purple pet, which lands them in the police station. Meanwhile, Dino, chased by the dino-catcher, ends up taking refuge in the same station and the family is happily reunited.

GROOM GLOOM

90

Production No.: P-90
Story: Herb Finn
Recording Date: 3/22/63
Air Date: 9/26/63

Voices:

Alan Reed	Fred, Old Fred
Mel Blanc	Barney, Old Barney,
	Bird, Dino,
	Old Dino, Needle Bird,
	1st and 2nd Ministers,
	Bird High Chair
Jean Vander Pyl	Wilma,
	Old Wilma, Pebbles
Bea Benaderet	Betty, Old Betty
Janet Waldo	Teenage Pebbles,
	Girl Bug
Don Messick	Duck, Boy Bug,
	Arnold, Big Arnold
John Stephenson	Baby Bird,
	3rd Minister,
	Old Slate, Rockhead,
	Buffalo

Fred falls asleep and dreams that Pebbles has grown up and is eloping with his archnemesis, Arnold, now "the world's richest newsboy." As they drive away, Arnold throws a newspaper and flattens Fred in the manner to which he has become accustomed, and worse, Pebbles throws a bouquet which turns into another paper and smacks him in the head. When Fred awakens, he snatches Pebbles back from Arnold, who is babysitting, and tells her to promise she won't grow up.

FRED'S MONKEYSHINES

91

Production No.: P-91
Story: Joanna Lee
Recording Date: 4/3/63
Air Date: 10/17/63

Voices:

Alan Reed	Fred
Mel Blanc	Barney, Turtle,
	Monkey, Dino,
	Gorilla
Jean Vander Pyl	Wilma,
	Pebbles, Lady
Bea Benaderet	Betty
Don Messick	Doctor, Bird,
	Elephant, Man,
	Kid, Manager
Doug Young	Cop, Beaver, Barker,
	Rocco, Father, Guy

After Wilma insists that he have his eyes examined, Fred inadvertently comes home wearing the optometrist's glasses, which give him the eyesight of Mr. Magoo. He kisses Dino, gives Wilma a bone, and takes a monkey to the circus, believing it to be Pebbles. The monkey climbs up onto the high wire and when Fred tries to save it, he ends up in the middle of a trapeze act. Removing his glasses, Fred faints and the monkey saves him.

THE FLINTSTONE CANARIES

92

Production No.: P-92
Story: Barry Blitzer
Recording Date: 4/5/63
Air Date: 10/24/63

Voices:

Alan Reed	Fred, Dinosaur
Mel Blanc	Barney, Dino,
	Elephant, Ape
Jean Vander Pyl	Wilma,
	Pebbles, Mouse,
	Girl Checker
Howard Morris	Chimp,
	Herman, Horse,
	Sam, Bird, Cop,
	General
John Stephenson	Foreman, Joe,
	Egg, Porcupine,
	Governor,
	Agency Man
Don Messick	Rabbit,
	Announcer, Fish,
	2nd Cop, Vic Stony

When Fred learns that the TV show, "Hum Along With Herman," is conducting a barbershop quartet contest, he immediately forms his own singing group. He is stymied by the group's inability to sing—until he discovers that Barney is a natural lead tenor. There is however one problem: Barney can only sing in the bathtub. Not letting this detail deter them, The Flintstone Canaries, led by Barney in his tub, audition for Herman and end up on TV—not in the show, but at the end, singing the virtues of the program's sponsor, Softsoap.

GLUE FOR TWO

93

Production No.: P-93

Story: Tony Benedict

Recording Date: 4/22/63

Air Date: 10/31/63

Voices:

Alan Reed	Fred
Mel Blanc	Barney, Elephant, Dino, Ethyl, Irving
Jean Vander Pyl	Wilma, Pebbles
Bea Benaderet	Betty, Nurse
Allan Melvin	Cop, Cat, Bird, Jane, Quartz, Doc

Fred invents a new soft drink that has all the sticking power of glue. When the stuff spills on Barney's bowling ball, which both men are holding, they literally become attached to one another. They drive to the gas station, where the "trained mechanic" tries to separate them, but nothing works. A consultation with Dr. Bonestitch also meets with no success. Finally Fred breaks the ball with a hammer, leaving Barney heartbroken because it was brand new. Fred, however, is excited by the strength of his formula until he discovers that the key ingredient was Rockbaum's Steel Glue, a product that is already on the market.

BIG LEAGUE FREDDIE

94

Production No.: P-94

Story: Walter Black

Recording Date: 4/25/63

Air Date: 11/7/63

Voices:

Alan Reed	Fred
Mel Blanc	Barney, Dino, Guy, Leo, Monkey
Jean Vander Pyl	Wilma, Pebbles
Bea Benaderet	Betty
Don Messick	Bird (Charlie), Roger, Elephant (Henry), Announcer, Warren
John Stephenson	Slate, Catcher, Umpire, 2nd Guy, Casey

When Fred gets knocked out playing for the Bedrock Quarry baseball team, he is replaced by Roger. Big league scouts from the Boulder City Giants are impressed by Roger's performance, but since he's wearing the Flintstone uniform, they mistakenly come to the Flintstone residence to sign Fred. The fact that Wilma, the Rubbles, and even Dino refuse to talk to Fred because he let Roger, the real star, miss his chance leaves him unperturbed, but when Pebbles "tells" him he's bad, Fred confesses to the scouts and Roger gets his big chance.

SLEEP ON, SWEET FRED

95

Production No.: P-95

Story: Joanna Lee

Recording Date: 4/30/63

Air Date: 11/21/63

Voices:

Alan Reed	Fred
Mel Blanc	Barney, Dino, Cop, Judge
Jean Vander Pyl	Wilma, Pebbles, Secretary
Bea Benaderet	Betty
Howard Morris	Mop Animal, Announcer, Peter, Al, Cop
John Stephenson	Dr. Firma, Slate, Sarge

Wilma and Betty use the sleep-teaching method on their husbands. The results are astounding and Fred and Barney become docile house-husbands. But they soon discover the brainwashing plan, and when the girls plant the suggestion to buy mink coats, they fake a plot to rob a mink warehouse. Wilma and Betty go to the warehouse to stop them, Pebbles throws a brick through the window, and they are all arrested, whereupon the judge sentences the wives to twenty days of serving their husbands breakfast in bed.

OLD LADY BETTY

96

Production No.: P-96

Story: Walter Black

Recording Date: 5/6/63

Air Date: 11/14/63

Voices:

Alan Reed	Fred
Mel Blanc	Barney, Dino, Bird Bath Bird, Turtle
Jean Vander Pyl	Wilma, Pebbles, Greta
Bea Benaderet	Betty
Allan Melvin	Stony, Sergeant, Elephant
Doug Young	Chopping Bird, Announcer, Cop

Betty decides to surprise Barney with a gift, and to earn money for it, she answers an ad for a job that calls for a kindly old lady. Disguising herself, she gets the position (purchasing small items with one hundred-dollar bills for another "old lady") and soon discovers her employers are counterfeiters. With Barney and the Flintstones waiting outside, Betty goes back to her job, hoping to nab the crooks, but they give her a real hundred-dollar bill and the police don't believe her story. Fred saves the day by leading Bedrock's finest to the crooks, and Betty buys Barney a new rocking chair.

DADDY'S LITTLE BEAUTY

 99

Production No.: P-99
Story: Herb Finn
Recording Date: 5/22/63
Air Date: 12/5/63

Voices:

Alan Reed	Fred
Mel Blanc	Barney, Dino, Horse
Jean Vander Pyl	Wilma,
	Pebbles, Girl
Bea Benaderet	Betty
Don Messick	Cuckoo Bird,
	Man, Bird,
	Monkey, 2nd Man,
	Doorman,
	P.A. Announcer
Daws Butler	Elephant,
	Photographer,
	Bus Driver, 1st Man,
	Mr. Goldbrick

Fred and Barney decide to enter Pebbles in a beauty contest. For the talent competition, Pebbles holds onto Dino's tail and blows kisses at the audience. Although all the other contestants are young women, not babies, Pebbles wins as Miss Beauty of the Future.

KLEPTOMANIAC PEBBLES

 97

Production No.: P-97
Story: Barry Blitzer
Recording Date: 5/14/63
Air Date: 11/28/63

Voices:

Alan Reed	Fred
Mel Blanc	Barney, Dino
Jean Vander Pyl	Wilma, Pebbles,
	Girl's Voice
Bea Benaderet	Betty
Daws Butler	Elephant,
	Pterodactyl, Hen,
	Clerk, Baffles,
	1st Detective,
	1st Traffic Cop
Howard Morris	Tortoise,
	Mammoth, Alligator,
	2nd Detective, Hotrock,
	Oyster, 2nd Traffic Cop

Out shopping with Pebbles, Fred has a hard time teaching her not to grab things off the shelves. At the ritzy Hot Rock jewelry store, the two run into Baffles Gravel, an international jewel thief. Spotted by a pair of detectives, Gravel plants a priceless diamond bracelet on Pebbles. At home, when Wilma finds the bracelet on the baby, Fred thinks she picked it up off the counter, and he and Barney go back to the store to return it. Since the shop is closed, the two decide to break in. Waiting detectives arrest the two as part of Baffles's gang, but the thief confesses rather have his name associated with Fred and Barney.

DADDIES ANONYMOUS

 98

Production No.: P-98
Story: Warren Foster
Recording Date: 5/21/63
Air Date: 12/12/63

Voices:

Alan Reed	Fred
Mel Blanc	Barney, Dino,
	Cat, Tiger
Jean Vander Pyl	Wilma,
	Pebbles, Norma
Bea Benaderet	Betty,
	Paper Boy, Alice
Howard Morris	Bird, 2nd Kid,
	2nd Monkey,
	Elmo, Elephant, Lucy
Don Messick	Bamm-Bamm, 1st Kid,
	1st Monkey, George
Doug Young	Cop, 1st Man,
	Alex, Chester

Fred and Barney join the exclusive Daddies Anonymous Club, where hen-pecked husbands play cards while their wives think they're out walking their babies. Rushing out at the end of a lucrative poker game, Fred and fellow member Elmo switch carriages—and babies—by mistake, and a hectic exchange ensues outside Pebbles's bedroom window. When the club is raided by the police, all the daddies and babies are hauled off to jail. The wives arrive to retrieve their children but refuse to post bail for the husbands.

BEDROCK HILLBILLIES

 100

Production No.: P-100
Story: Herb Finn
Recording Date: 6/11/63
Air Date: 1/16/64

Voices:

Alan Reed	Fred, 1st Man,
	Worker
Mel Blanc	Barney, Dino,
	Zack, Pig
Jean Vander Pyl	Wilma, Pebbles
Bea Benaderet	Betty, Ma
Doug Young	Minister, 2nd Man,
	Airmail Bird
June Foray	Old Woman, Ma,
	Granny, Secretary,
	2nd Dinosaur,
	Monkey
Howard Morris	Percy, Pa,
	Slab, Possum,
	1st Dinosaur,
	Attendant
John Stephenson	Shystone,
	Mr. Slate, Fish

Fred receives word that he has inherited a shack in the mountains because the last of his hillbilly relations has just died. Arriving in the hills, the Flintstones and Rubbles are greeted by a hail of bullets and soon discover they have also inherited a hundred-year-old feud with the Hatrock family. The feud is forgotten when Fred rescues a Hatrock baby—until he makes an insulting comment about the hillbillies' great-great-grandma and the Hatrocks gleefully begin shooting anew.

LITTLE BAMM-BAMM

101

Production No.: P-101
Story: Warren Foster
Recording Date: 6/12/63
Air Date: 10/3/63

Voices:

Alan Reed	Fred, Turtle
Mel Blanc	Barney, Dino, Stony
Jean Vander Pyl	Wilma,
	Pebbles, Woman
Bea Benaderet	Betty, Old Lady
Don Messick	Bamm-Bamm, Bird,
	Judge, Perry Masonry
Hal Smith	Cat, Orderly,
	Mr. Berger,
	Driver, Bailiff

Desperately wanting a baby, the Rubbles wish on a star and awaken the next morning to discover tow-headed Bamm-Bamm on their doorstep. They fall in love with him and decide to adopt, but the Welfare Bureau informs the couple that the baby has already been promised to wealthy Mr. Pronto Berger, who has retained the famous attorney Perry Masonry to handle the court case. The Rubbles are no match for Masonry and lose the case. As they are leaving the court heartbroken, Mr. Berger learns his wife is pregnant and gives custody of Bamm-Bamm to the Rubbles.

PEEK-A-BOO CAMERA

102

Production No.: P-102
Story: Barry Blitzer
Recording Date: 6/21/63
Air Date: 12/19/63

Voices:

Alan Reed	Fred
Mel Blanc	Barney, Dino, Tiger
Jean Vander Pyl	Wilma,
	Mrs. Poobah
Bea Benaderet	Betty, Lady
Howard Morris	TV Announcer,
	Monkey, Cat,
	3rd Buffalo,
	Emcee, Bird #1
Doug Young	Tortoise, Cop,
	Poobah
Hal Smith	Rocky Genial,
	2nd Buffalo,
	4th Buffalo, Shelly,
	Baseball Fan, Bird #2
Al Melvin	Quartz, Owner,
	Sportscaster, Sleuth,
	Doorman, 1st Buffalo

When the Grand Poobah orders up a bachelor party for one of the Lodge members, Fred and Barney tell the girls they have to skip celebrating the Flintstones' anniversary to pay their last respects to an old friend. The party shifts to a night club and Fred and Barney put on an impromptu act with the chorus girls, unaware that Rocky Genial, host of Peek-A-Boo Camera, is filming the whole show. The boys manage to prevent their wives from seeing the program, but it's such a hit that it is rerun on TV the following week—and this time Betty and Wilma are watching.

ANN-MARGROCK PRESENTS

103

Production No.: P-103
Story: Harvey Bullock/
R. Saffian
Recording Date: 6/28/63
Air Date: 9/19/63

Voices:

Alan Reed	Fred
Mel Blanc	Barney
Jean Vander Pyl	Wilma,
	Pebbles
John Stephenson	Sponsor,
	1st Guy, Slate,
	Turtle,
	Dr. Ben Cavity
Daws Butler	2nd Guy, Lulu Belle,
	Harry, Bird,
	Porcupine
Howard Morris	Bobby,
	Parrot, Announcer
Ann Margret	Ann-Margrock

Ann-Margrock, voiced by real-life celebrity Ann-Margret, arrives in town to perform at the new Bedrock Bowl ampitheater. Told by her manager to find someplace quiet to stay until showtime, she is driving down Cobblestone Lane when her car suffers a flat tire in front of the Flintstone home. When she comes in to use the phone, Fred and Wilma hire her as a babysitter for Pebbles. Enchanted by the tyke, she accepts. After Ann sings Pebbles to sleep with a lullaby, she helps Fred and Barney rehearse an act for the Bowl show. Unaware of the identity of their houseguest, they invite her to be part of their act and at showtime are stunned to learn that Annie is Ann-Margrock. They are delighted when she invites them to perform onstage with her.

TEN LITTLE FLINTSTONES

104

Production No.: P-104
Story: Tony Benedict
Recording Date: 7/8/63
Air Date: 1/2/64

Voices:

Alan Reed	Fred
Mel Blanc	Barney, Dino, Parrot
Jean Vander Pyl	Wilma,
	Pebbles
Bea Benaderet	Betty,
	Secretary
Don Messick	Reporter,
	Master, Bamm-Bamm,
	Rooster, Rockwell,
	Robot Fred
John Stephenson	Pelican, Slate

Ten robots from another planet land in Bedrock to begin their conquest of Earth. Mirror images of Fred, they wreak havoc smacking Barney with a sandwich, flirting with girls in front of Wilma, and antagonizing Mr. Slate. The master of the robots, realizing that Fred is aware of the plan, recalls his machine men and they take off, leaving poor Fred to explain his behavior.

ONCE UPON A COWARD

105

Production No.: P-105

Story: N/A

Recording Dates: 7/12/63 and 7/19/63

Air Date: 12/26/63

Voices:

Alan Reed	Fred
Mel Blanc	Barney, Mathilda, Dino
Jean Vander Pyl	Wilma, Pebbles, 1st Woman, Lady
Bea Benaderet	Betty
Doug Young	Bird, 1st Cop (O'Rockly), Fight Announcer, 2nd Guy, 4th Guy
Hal Smith	Holdup Man, Harvey, 3rd Guy, Chief, Sonny
Janet Waldo	Mrs. Sitstone, 2nd Woman, 3rd Woman
Don Messick	Bamm-Bamm, Arnold, TV Announcer, 1st Guy, Shaley

After Fred has been robbed without putting up a fight, he goes out of his way to prove he's not a coward. He tries to box with Sonny Dempstone and to tame a tiger at the circus. Later, while bowling, he recognizes the voice of the holdup man and mows him down with a bowling ball. The newspapers hail Fred as a man of valor, and his honor is redeemed.

FRED EL TERRIFICO

106

Production No.: P-106

Story: Joanna Lee

Recording Date: 7/19/63

Air Date: 1/9/64

Voices:

Alan Reed	Fred
Mel Blanc	Barney, Dino, Popo
Jean Vander Pyl	Wilma, Pebbles, Shala
Bea Benaderet	Betty
Don Messick	Bamm-Bamm, Voice on Speaker, Harvey, Torero, Fan, Turtle
Janet Waldo	Mrs. Slaghoople, Mildred, Hostess
Howard Morris	Rockoff, Bird, Official, Proprietor, Joe

Vacationing in Rockapulco, Fred gets into trouble when a pair of international crooks befriends him and plants a million dollars in stolen diamonds on him to be carried across the border. When Fred wanders into a bullring by mistake, he ends up fighting the huge beast, impressing the glamorous lady thief. Wilma becomes jealous and breaks the jewel-filled maraca, where the diamonds were hidden, and they go flying. Fred gets a cash reward for the capture of the thieves, but is then arrested in customs for not declaring the money.

FLINTSTONE AND THE LION

107

Production No.: P-107

Story: Tony Benedict

Recording Date: 7/29/63

Air Date: 1/23/64

Voices:

Alan Reed	Fred
Mel Blanc	Barney, Dino, Cub, Lion
Jean Vander Pyl	Wilma, Pebbles, Edie
Bea Benaderet	Betty
Elliot Field	Bear, Mailman, Mortar
Don Messick	Bamm-Bamm, Cat, Salesman, Loudmouth, Guy, Guard

Fred befriends a kitten while on a fishing trip and decides to make a pet of it. He's eaten out of house and home when the kitten grows up into a full-fledged lion, but he refuses to believe it's more than a "little old alley cat." Ultimately Fred does become convinced, and he tries repeatedly to set the animal free but it won't leave. Zookeepers use a winsome lady lion as bait and carry the lion off with his new love. Before long, the lions return to the Flintstones' home to show off their babies.

CAVE SCOUT JAMBOREE

108

Production No.: P-108

Story: Warren Foster

Recording Date: 8/5/63

Air Date: 1/30/64

Voices:

Alan Reed	Fred
Mel Blanc	Barney, Dino, Lulu Belle, Bird
Jean Vander Pyl	Wilma, Pebbles
Bea Benaderet	Betty
Don Messick	Bamm-Bamm, Charlie, Mailbird, 1st Man, 2nd Boy, 4th Boy
John Stephenson	Slate, 2nd Man, Scoutmaster
Dick Beals	1st Boy, 3rd Boy, 5th Boy

The Flintstones and Rubbles go camping at secluded Shangri La-De-Da and pitch their tents for the night. In the morning the couples awaken to discover they are surrounded by a scout jamboree. At first dismayed, they end up having a great time. The scouts perform daily good deeds for Betty and Wilma, and Fred and Barney become the hit of the night time festivities. The scouts have so much fun that they take Fred up on his offer to visit in Bedrock, and they move their jamboree to the Flintstones' backyard.

LADIES NIGHT AT THE LODGE

109

Production No.: P-109

Story: Herb Finn

Recording Date: 8/16/63

Air Date: 2/13/64

Voices:

Alan Reed	Fred
Mel Blanc	Barney,
	Dino, Big Guy
Jean Vander Pyl	Wilma, Pebbles,
	Mrs. Sitstone
Bea Benaderet	Betty
Howard Morris	Voice, Treasurer,
	Turtle, Bird,
	Scotchman,
	Timid Man
Doug Young	Poobah, 1st Voice,
	Doorman
Don Messick	Bamm-Bamm,
	Quartz, 2nd Voice,
	Pig, Member

Anxious to join the Water Buffalos, Wilma and Betty disguise themselves as guys and gain entrance to a Lodge meeting. But when they are subjected to the club's initiation ritual—being paddled by the Buffalos, tossed into a pool of mud in a tug of war, and hosed down with a mastodon trunk, they decide it's a man's world after all. In the midst of the three-legged race, the girls rush off the stage, out the door, and head for home.

ROOM FOR TWO

110

Production No.: P-110

Story: Tony Benedict

Recording Date: 8/29/63

Air Date: 2/6/64

Voices:

Alan Reed	Fred
Mel Blanc	Barney,
	Dino, Dinosaur
Bea Benaderet	Betty
Jean Vander Pyl	Wilma, Pebbles
Don Messick	Bamm-Bamm,
	Porcupine, Monkey,
	Ratchet, Squirrel
Doug Young	Beaver,
	Grand Poobah, Cop
Hal Smith	Bird, Joe Rockhead,
	Guy, Cat,
	Phonograph Bird

Fred wants to add a new room to the house and enlists Barney's assistance in building it. The new addition is completed with the boys' friendship intact, but when Joe Rockhead beats Fred in the Water Buffalo of the Year competition—with Barney having cast the deciding vote—the feud is on. When Barney learns half the room extends onto his property, he takes possession of it, and a wild war erupts. Barney sets a lion to guard his half and Fred fences off his portion; Barney throws a loud party and Fred hooks up every speaker in town to blast his buddy's eardrums with music. The feud finally ends when Bamm-Bamm, fed up with all the fighting, tears down the room.

REEL TROUBLE

111

Production No.: P-111

Story: Barry Blitzer

Recording Date: 9/4/63

Air Date: 2/20/64

Voices:

Alan Reed	Fred
Mel Blanc	Barney,
	Dino, Fingers
Jean Vander Pyl	Wilma, Pebbles
Bea Benaderet	Betty
Don Messick	Bamm-Bamm,
	1st Buffalo,
	3rd Buffalo,
	Boss, Guard, Radio
Doug Young	Poobah,
	TV Announcer,
	Cop, 2nd Buffalo,
	Clerk

Fred becomes a home movie maniac, insisting on running his footage of Pebbles seven nights a week to the infinite boredom of the Rubbles and the Water Buffalos. Later, outside the art museum, he accidentally films a couple of thieves. The crooks offer to pay for the movie, but Fred refuses to sell. He then learns their identity and flees with his camera, but the Rubbles, believing he wants to show them more movies, won't let him in their house. Later, when the bad guys get beaned with Fred's bowling ball, he ties them up and makes them watch his home movies.

BACHELOR DAZE

112

Production No.: P-112

Story: Ralph Goodman;

Teleplay by Herb Finn

Recording Date: 9/26/63

Air Date: 3/5/64

Voices:

Alan Reed	Fred
Mel Blanc	Barney,
	Dino, Stonyface
Jean Vander Pyl	Wilma, Pebbles
Bea Benaderet	Betty
Don Messick	Bamm-Bamm,
	Arnold, Clock Bird,
	2nd Horn,
	Bird, Driver
Howard Morris	Baggage Monkey,
	Reggie, Horn Bird,
	Actor, Dragon,
	Alligator
Janet Waldo	Doris,
	Actress (Pamela),
	Mrs. Slaghoople

Wilma and Betty reminisce over their first meeting with Fred and Barney at the famed Honeyrock Hotel, and the story flashes back to the girls sitting in a fancy car, imagining what it would feel like to be rich and famous. Meanwhile, Fred and Barney are parking a wealthy guest's limo in the same lot. The pairs meet and it's love at first sight—with the girls believing the boys are millionaires and the boys thinking the girls are heiresses. Later, at a costume ball, they discover the truth—the girls are actually waitresses; the boys, bellhops. Wilma's mother is terribly disappointed, but it's too late; the couples have already decided that they're made for each other.

SON OF ROCKZILLA

113

Production No.: P-113

Story: Barry Blitzer

Recording Date: 9/30/63

Air Date: 2/27/64

Voices:

Alan Reed	Fred
Mel Blanc	Barney, Dino, Parrot
Jean Vander Pyl	Wilma, Pebbles
Bea Benaderet	Betty, Octopus
Gerry Johnson	Henry's Woman, 2nd Woman, Selma
Hal Smith	Father, 2nd Cop, 1st Announcer, Doris, Boy, Fiendish
Doug Young	Guy, Bunkly, 1st Cop, 1st Ape, Sergeant
Don Messick	Bamm-Bamm, Editor, 2nd Ape, 2nd Announcer, Waiter, Rabbit, Arnold
Janet Waldo	Stout Woman, 1st Woman, Fran

Hired to do publicity for Fiendish Films, Fred wears a monster costume to attract attention to the horror movie *Son of Rockzilla*. When he goes to the zoo to learn monster technique from Doris the Finkasaurus, she escapes. At the same time that the studio publicity man reports a monster loose in town, the catch on Fred's suit gets stuck and he can't get the head off. He bumps into Doris, who falls in love with him and chases him all over town, as do the police. Finally Fred gets the costume off and Doris transfers her affections to Barney, who leads her back to the zoo.

OPERATION SWITCHOVER

114

Production No.: P-114

Story: Joanna Lee

Recording Date: 10/2/63

Air Date: 3/12/64

Voices:

Alan Reed	Fred
Mel Blanc	Barney, Dino
Jean Vander Pyl	Wilma, Pebbles, 2nd Woman
Bea Benaderet	Betty
Don Messick	Bamm-Bamm, Dusting Bird, Charlie, Alligator, 2nd Man, Flash
Janet Waldo	1st Woman, Hedda, Girl
Doug Young	Clock Bird, 1st Man, Joe
John Stephenson	Hat Bird, Slate, 3rd Man

When Wilma becomes a finalist for Good Cavekeeping Magazine's Housewife of the Year award, Fred decides a housewife's life is easy and the two exchange jobs for a day. At the quarry, Wilma has trouble running the dino-crane and repeatedly flattens Mr. Slate with boulders. Meanwhile, Fred irons a hole through all the clothes, breaks the dishes, and overboils so much rice that it floods the house and yard. When the magazine editor calls to say she's arriving in twenty minutes to take pictures of Wilma, Fred organizes Barney and his poker buddies to help him become housewife of the year. Wearing a wig and lipstick, he greets the editor while Barney prepares hors d'oeuvres from Dino's dog food. Fred wins first prize, admits he wouldn't have Wilma's job for anything, and the couple serves one another breakfast in bed.

PEBBLES'S BIRTHDAY PARTY

115

Production No.: P-115

Story: Tony Benedict

Recording Date: 3/3/64

Air Date: 10/8/64

Voices:

Alan Reed	Fred
Mel Blanc	Barney, Attendant
Jean Vander Pyl	Wilma, Pebbles
Gerry Johnson	Betty, Wife
Don Messick	Bamm-Bamm, Cat, Gopher, 2nd Guy, 1st Kid, 3rd Kid, Musician
John Stephenson	Bird, Clown, 2nd Kid, Neighbor, Sarge, 1st Guy
Doug Young	Grand Poobah, 3rd Guy, Clerk, Musician, Dispatcher

Fred gets into trouble when he tries to arrange a birthday party for Pebbles and a party for his Lodge brothers on the same night. The confused caterer sends Rocko the Clown to the Lodge and the Boulderette dancing girls to Pebbles's party. The kids end up playing poker while the rowdy Lodge members try to play pin the tail on the clown. The police are called to the Flintstone home and everyone is herded into the paddy wagon. When the police arrive to arrest the Water Buffalos for disturbing the peace—they're trying to attack Fred for ruining their party—the Boulderettes leap out of the wagon as the Buffalos crowd in.

HOP HAPPY

116

Production No.: P-116

Story: Warren Foster

Recording Date: 3/10/64

Air Date: 9/17/64

Voices:

Alan Reed	Fred, Pig
Mel Blanc	Barney, Dino, Cop, Mouse
Jean Vander Pyl	Wilma, Pebbles
Gerry Johnson	Betty
Don Messick	Bamm-Bamm, Bird, Clerk, Animal, Bird #2, Hoppy, Mouse, Siren

Barney takes Bamm-Bamm to the Bedrock Pet Shop to pick out a pet. Bamm-Bamm falls in love with a hopparoo and they take it home. Hoppy fetches, babysits Bamm-Bamm, and boxes Fred. Miffed at being beaten by the animal, Fred decides to move, until the Rubbles invite them on a picnic. At the park, the Flintstones and Rubbles become trapped in a car that rolls over the edge of a cliff and strands them on a limb. Hoppy hops to the police station, summons the entire force—plus the fire department—to rescue them and gets his picture in the paper.

CINDERELLAST ONE

117

Production No.: P-117

Story: Tony Benedict

Recording Date: 3/19/64

Air Date: 10/22/64

Voices:

Alan Reed	Fred
Mel Blanc	Barney,
	Bird, Alligator
Jean Vander Pyl	Wilma, Pebbles,
	Fairy Godmother
Gerry Johnson	Betty, Mrs. Slate,
	Secretary, 2nd Gal
Don Messick	Bamm-Bamm, Shale,
	Stucco, Butler, Leader,
	1st Guy, Hoppy,
	4th Guy, 5th Guy
John Stephenson	Stony, Silt,
	Slate, 1st Guy

Fred is upset when he learns he's the only employee not invited to a party at which Mr. Slate will decide who is most suited to be the new foreman. After reading "Cinderelly" to Pebbles and Bamm-Bamm, he goes to bed and is awakened by a fairy godmother who takes him to the party in a pumpkin limousine. He's a big hit, but wakes to find that it was just a dream. The next day, when Mr. Slate tells Fred he was recommended by one of the top brass at the party and is now the new foreman—just as in his dream—he concludes that fairy godmothers do exist.

MONSTER FRED

118

Production No.: P-118

Story: Not Available

Recording Date: 4/3/64

Air Date: 9/24/64

Voices:

Alan Reed	Fred
Mel Blanc	Barney, Dino,
	2nd Guy, Bat
Jean Vander Pyl	Wilma, Pebbles
Gerry Johnson	Betty
Doug Young	1st Guy, Zero,
	Pterodactyl,
	Dracuslab
Don Messick	Bamm-Bamm,
	Hoppy, Turtle,
	Cat, Barking
Alan Melvin	Len Frankenstone
Howard Morris	Doc

Barney's prediction that bowling lane thirteen is unlucky proves correct when Fred is conked on the head with a bowling ball. Regaining consciousness, Fred thinks he's a baby. Barney takes him to Dr. Sigrock Freep, who only performs magic tricks with his patient, so they move on to Dr. Frankenstone who has been conducting experiments on switching the personalities of animals. The doctor's treatment results in Fred assuming Dino's personality and vice versa. Trying to remedy his error, Frankenstone accidentally switches Fred's personality with Barney's. When Wilma and Betty arrive and try to help, Fred is conked on the head again and starts calling for his mommy.

ITTY BITTY FREDDY

119

Production No.: P-119

Story: Not Available

Recording Date: 4/15/64

Air Date: 10/1/64

Voices:

Alan Reed	Fred
Mel Blanc	Barney, Dino,
	2nd Bird
Jean Vander Pyl	Wilma,
	Pebbles, Girl
Gerry Johnson	Betty
Don Messick	Bamm-Bamm,
	Guy, Mouse,
	Dog, Cat,
	Announcer
Doug Young	1st Bird, Doc,
	2nd Doc
Daws Butler	Agent,
	Ed Sullystone

While playing inventor in the garage, Fred comes up with Fred-O-Cal, a revolutionary new reducing formula, and promptly reduces himself to miniature size. Seeing opportunity in his pal's predicament, Barney answers an ad for new novelty acts for the Ed Sullystone Show, and with Rubble as the ventriloquist and Flintstone as the dummy, the two are a hit, until Fred returns to normal size during the broadcast. Back home, Fred promises to give up inventing and pours his potion out the window, into Dino's bowl. The purple pet drinks the stuff and becomes tiny as well.

BEDROCK RODEO ROUND-UP

120

Production No.: P-120

Story: Not Available

Recording Date: 4/16/64

Air Date: 10/15/64

Voices:

Alan Reed	Fred
Mel Blanc	Barney, Dino,
	Stegosaurus, Car
Jean Vander Pyl	Wilma, Pebbles
Gerry Johnson	Betty
Don Messick	Bamm-Bamm,
	Dinosaur, Hoppy,
	Announcer, Brady
Alvin Melvin	Bony Hurdle

Wilma's old pal, Bony Hurdle, comes to town for the Bedrock Rodeo and pays a visit to the Flintstones. When Pebbles starts calling him "Dada," Fred's jealousy gets the better of him and he joins the rodeo in hopes of winning back Pebbles's love by defeating Bony. Fred's inept riding wows the crowd, who think he's a great acrobatic clown. The rodeo manager offers Fred a lucrative contract, but having already won Pebbles's adoration, he turns it down.

A HAUNTED HOUSE IS NOT A HOME

121

Production No.: P-121
Story: Not Available
Recording Date: 4/21/64
Air Date: 10/29/64

Voices:

Alan Reed	Fred
Mel Blanc	Barney, Dino, Wormstone
Jean Vander Pyl	Wilma, Pebbles
Gerry Johnson	Betty
Don Messick	Bamm-Bamm, Bird, Hoppy, Blackstone, Potrock, Cuckoo
Hal Smith	Creepers, Horace, Giggles

Fred's uncle, J. Giggles Flintstone, passes away and names him sole heir to his estate, but to receive the inheritance, the will stipulates that Fred must spend one night in Giggles's spooky mansion. Barney agrees to stay with Fred, and during the night, Giggles's servants unsuccessfully attempt to scare the two away. In the morning, a very alive Giggles appears, and explains that he was just testing Fred to see if he would be a worthy heir. This makes Fred so angry that he maniacally pursues Giggles, thereby ruining any chances of inheriting the estate.

DR. SINISTER

122

Production No.: P-122
Story: Not Available
Recording Date: 4/22/64
Air Date: 11/5/64

Voices:

Alan Reed	Fred
Mel Blanc	Barney, Boss, Dr. Sinister
Jean Vander Pyl	Wilma, Pebbles, 2nd Girl, Madam Yes
Gerry Johnson	Betty, Girl
Doug Young	Jay Bondrock, Guy (Street), Guard, Strong Guy, Bird
Don Messick	Bamm-Bamm, Screen Guy, Thug, Pit Guy

Fred and Barney become embroiled in an international plot with Madam Yes, a beautiful spy, and Dr. Sinister, who seeks world domination. After escaping certain death within the doctor's volcanic island lair, Fred and Barney discover his World Destruction Machine (patent pending). They jump off a cliff and swim away just as the island blows up, but when they get home, Betty and Wilma refuse to believe their story.

THE GRUESOMES

123

Production No.: P-123
Story: Not Available
Recording Date: 5/1/64
Air Date: 11/12/64

Voices:

Alan Reed	Fred, Animal
Mel Blanc	Barney, Dino, Bat
Jean Vander Pyl	Wilma, Pebbles
Gerry Johnson	Betty
Don Messick	Bamm-Bamm, Realtor, Goblin, Bird, Grasshopper, Gila Monster
Howard Morris	Weirdly, Spider, Flower, Head, TV Announcer
Naomi Lewis	Creepella

Weirdly Gruesome, his wife Creepella, and their son, Goblin, move into Tombstone Manor, next door to the Flintstones. Despite the family's strange appearance, and their stranger behavior, Fred and Wilma are determined to be nice neighbors. But when Fred and Barney babysit Gobby, he and his weird pets—including a man-eating iguana, octopus, and plant—make for a hairraising evening. When the parents finally return home, Fred decides to move away—until, that is, he discovers that the Gruesomes have their own TV show.

THE MOST BEAUTIFUL BABY IN BEDROCK

124

Production No.: P-124
Story: Not Available
Recording Date: 5/11/64
Air Date: 11/19/64

Voices:

Alan Reed	Fred, Waldo (Dog), Dinosaur Roar
Mel Blanc	Barney, Dino, Elephant
Jean Vander Pyl	Wilma, Pebbles
Gerry Johnson	Betty, Julietta, Tired Woman, Woman Guest
Don Messick	Bamm-Bamm, Rockeo, Pizza Bird, Rockhead, Hoppy, Moe, 2nd Guest, Woodpecker
Doug Young	Capulet, Poobah, Gravel, Mop Bird, Muscles, Jack
Henry Corden	1st Guest, Doctor, Monte, Shale, Manny

After Wilma and Betty force Fred and Barney to see *Rockeo and Julietta* at the movies, the boys critize the plot, saying two families would never engage in such a silly feud. But when the Water Buffalos hold a beautiful baby contest, Fred and Barney begin fighting over whose baby is more adorable. Soon the wives are drawn into the fray and a small war breaks out. At the height of the quarrel, they discover that Pebbles and Bamm-Bamm have disappeared. When the kids are found, the parents realize they ran away because of the bickering, and soon all is back to normal.

DINO AND JULIET

125

Production No.: P-125
Story: Not Available
Recording Date: 5/21/64
Air Date: 11/26/64

Voices:

Alan Reed — Fred, Steam Bird
Mel Blanc — Barney, Dino, Doctor
Jean Vander Pyl — Wilma, Pebbles
Gerry Johnson — Betty
Henry Corden — Loudrock
Don Messick — Bamm-Bamm, Hoppy, Elephant, Dog, Clerk

When the Flintstones' new neighbor, Mr. Loudrock, proves to be an overbearing brute, he and Fred begin to feud. Fred enlists Dino to protect him from Loudrock's pet, but instead, Dino falls in love with it. The feud continues until the two discover that Loudrock's pet is expecting and Dino is the father. Soon fifteen pink puppies arrive, and Fred and Loudrock become buddies.

KING FOR A NIGHT

126

Production No.: P-126
Story: Not Available
Recording Date: 5/26/64
Air Date: 12/3/64

Voices:

Alan Reed — Fred, King
Mel Blanc — Barney, Dino
Jean Vander Pyl — Wilma, Pebbles, Joan
Gerry Johnson — Betty, Waitress, Guyla
Don Messick — Bamm-Bamm, Rosencave, Joe, Bill, Bellboy, Boy
Nancy Wible — Wednesday
Henry Corden — Gildenstone

The King of Stonesylvania comes to Bedrock with his assistants, Rosencave and Gildenstone, to secure a ten million-dollar loan for his country. Tired of his kingly duties, he shaves off his beard and leaves the hotel. Searching for him, Rosencave and Gildenstone come upon Fred, a mirror image of the royal man. Fred accepts three thousand krubeks to impersonate the king. Meanwhile, Barney runs into the king and, thinking he's Fred under a delusion, tries to save him from himself. Betty and Wilma find the real Fred dancing at a ball and become infuriated. When the real king returns to the hotel, he, along with Fred, the girls, and Barney, get caught up in a mad chase. Finally, everything is straightened out, the king resumes his identity, and Fred discovers that the three thousand Stonesylvania krubeks are worth only $3.95 in Bedrock currency.

INDIANROCK-OLIS 500

127

Production No.: P-127
Story: Rance Howard
Recording Date: 6/12/64
Air Date: 12/10/64

Voices:

Alan Reed — Fred, Friend
Mel Blanc — Barney, Dino, Turtle
Jean Vander Pyl — Wilma, Pebbles
Gerry Johnson — Betty
Don Messick — Bamm-Bamm, Hoppy, Sewing Bird, Phone Monkey, Race Announcer
John Stephenson — Slate, Rocky, TV Announcer, Flagman

When Barney builds a race car in his garage, he and Fred enter it in the Indianrockolis 500 with Fred as the driver. Posing as Goggles Pisano, a foreign driver, Fred wows the crowd with his driving feats. Unfortunately, his wheels disintegrate and he ends up crossing the finish line on foot, carrying the car. Not only is he disqualified, but when Mr. Slate discovers Fred's at the race instead of at work, he fires him. When Fred and Barney are paid $5,000 to make a TV pitch for Flintrock wheels, however, Slate wants to get in on the commercial, and Fred is rehired.

ADOBE DICK

128

Production No.: P-128
Story: Barry Blitzer
Recording Date: 6/4/64
Air Date: 12/17/64

Voices:

Alan Reed — Fred, #2 Member, #3 Member
Mel Blanc — Barney, Dino, Octopus
Jean Vander Pyl — Wilma, Pebbles
Gerry Johnson — Betty, Dame
Don Messick — Bamm-Bamm, Hoppy, #1 Fly, Seagull, Camera Bird, Announcer
Doug Young — #2 Fly, Horn Bird, Grand Poobah, 1st Chimp, Fish
Hal Smith — #1 Member, 2nd Chimp, Captain Blah, Whale

Fred and Barney go fishing with the Water Buffalos aboard the HMS Bountystone. Having no luck, the two go off in search of a better fishing spot and land on a small island, which turns out to be the feared whale-asaurus Adobe Dick. Trying to escape, they row into what appears to be a cave, only to find themselves inside the huge creature's mouth. Lighting a fire inside the whale, Fred and Barney beach Adobe Dick, then tickle him until he opens his mouth, allowing them to run out. Barney takes a photo of Fred standing next to the whaleasaurus to prove their fish story, but when the film gets developed, they discover that Barney has taken a close-up of his own thumb.

FRED'S FLYING LESSON

129

Production No.: P-129

Story: Rick Mittelman

Recording Date: 6/18/64

Air Date: 1/1/65

Voices:

Alan Reed	Fred, Pelican
Mel Blanc	Barney,
	Dino, Monkey
Jean Vander Pyl	Wilma,
	Pebbles,
	Kitty Rockhawk
Gerry Johnson	Betty,
	Hilda Rockmouth,
	1st Dame, 2nd Dame,
	3rd Dame
Don Messick	Bamm-Bamm,
	Hoppy, Oscar,
	Kettle Bird, Corporal,
	Dodo Bird, Siren Bird
Doug Young	Charlie,
	Control Tower,
	1st Bird, Poobah
Hal Smith	2nd Bird,
	General, Pine Cone

Fred wins a free lesson at the Bedrock Flying School. When his beautiful instructor, Kitty Rockhawk, convinces him to sign up for the five-lesson plan, he starts dreaming of a career as an airline pilot. Completing all five lessons in one day, Fred returns the following morning for his solo flight, with Barney as his copilot. Trouble begins when Fred flies over the restricted area of an army base and Barney drops a boulder on the radar room, which the soldiers think is a bomb. When the soldiers begin shooting at the plane, Fred pulls the ejector handle by mistake and is thrown out. Although he talks Barney down by radio and Kitty praises them both, Fred decides that flying is not for him.

FRED'S SECOND CAR

130

Production No.: P-130

Story: Rance Howard

Recording Date: 7/2/64

Air Date: 1/8/65

Voices:

Alan Reed	Fred, Shorty
Mel Blanc	Barney,
	Dino, Herman
Jean Vander Pyl	Wilma,
	Pebbles
Gerry Johnson	Betty
Don Messick	Bamm-Bamm,
	Hoppy, Pterodactyl,
	Toaster Bird,
	Auctioneer, 1st Cop
Henry Corden	Big Sparkle,
	Stoolie Pigeon,
	Charlie
Doug Young	Egg Monkey,
	Man, Linko

With both Wilma and Betty using the family cars, Fred decides it's time to get a second vehicle. He buys one at a police auction, but learns that a gang of thieves is also interested in the car. They believe it has a cache of jewels hidden inside. Fred and Barney are chased by the crooks and captured. Fred sends Dino for help, but in the meantime, he and Barney engineer an escape. When the thieves are flattened by the car's wheel, which actually does contain stolen diamonds, the boys turn them over to the police, who have been summoned by Dino and the girls.

CHRISTMAS FLINTSTONE

131

Production No.: P-131

Story: Warren Foster

Recording Date: 7/9/64

Air Date: 12/25/64

Voices:

Alan Reed	Fred, Chimney Pipe
Mel Blanc	Barney, Dino, Mr.
	Macyrock
Jean Vander Pyl	Wilma,
	Pebbles
Gerry Johnson	Betty,
	Woman, Speaker,
	Girl, Small girl,
	Matron
Hal Smith	Guy, Bird, Animal,
	Voice, Santa Claus
Don Messick	Bamm-Bamm,
	Hoppy, Stairs,
	2nd Kid,
	TV Announcer,
	2nd Elf
Dick Beals	Kid, 3rd Kid,
	1st Elf, Boy

Fred takes a job at the Macyrock Department Store to earn money for Christmas gifts, but he is so inept, the boss is compelled to fire him. At the last moment, Fred is asked to fill in for the store's Santa. He is such a hit that the real Santa, sick in bed at the North Pole, sends two elves, Twinky and Blinky, to whisk him off as a substitute Saint Nick. Fred successfully circles the globe delivering gifts—a large number of which are Pebbles dolls—but forgets to drop presents at his own house. Arriving home empty-handed, Fred discovers that the real Santa has made a personal appearance in his living room and has saved the day.

THE HATROCKS AND THE GRUESOMES

132

Production No.: P-132

Story: Herb Finn/

Alan Dinehart

Recording Date: 7/16/64

Air Date: 1/22/65

Voices:

Alan Reed	Fred, Porker, Ghastly
Mel Blanc	Barney, Dino, Zack
Jean Vander Pyl	Wilma,
	Pebbles, Creepella
Gerry Johnson	Betty,
	Granny, Girl
Don Messick	Bamm-Bamm,
	Hoppy, Turtle, Boy,
	Plant, Gobbie,
	Record Bird
Howard Morris	Jethro Hatrock,
	Slab, Waiter,
	Percy, Boy, Weirdly

When the Hatrocks come to Bedrock, Fred fears the old Hatrock-Flintstone feud will erupt, but the hillbillies are only planning a quick stop-over on their way to the World's Fair. When Fred idly remarks, "Too bad you can't stay longer," they decide to do just that. The visitors proceed to eat Fred and Wilma out of house and home, and Fred calls on the Gruesomes to help scare them off. Unfortunately, the Hatrocks are only amused. Finally Fred discovers the Hatrocks can't stand "bug" music, and the Flintstones, Rubbles, and Gruesomes don Beatles' wigs and sing, "I said yeah, yeah, yeah," until the Hatrocks flee for the hills.

TIME MACHINE

133

Production No.: P-133
Story: William Idelson/
Samuel Bobrick
Recording Date: 7/15/64
Air Date: 1/15/65

Voices:

Alan Reed	Fred
Mel Blanc	Barney, Gorilla, 2nd
	Lionosauruses
Jean Vander Pyl	Wilma,
	Pebbles,
	Little Girl, Queen
Gerry Johnson	Betty,
	Woman, Leonore,
	2nd Woman, Mabel
Don Messick	Bamm-Bamm,
	Boy Child,
	Monkeysaurus,
	Beaver, Inventor
Howard Morris	Hippo,
	Bird, Duck,
	1st Lionosauruses,
	Sailor, Squire
John Stephenson	Attendant,
	Tiberius, Nero,
	Arthur,
	Astronomer, Cop
Henry Corden	Brutus,
	Guard, Columbus,
	Knight, Clerk

While the Flintstones and Rubbles are visiting the World's Fair, an inventor persuades them to try an untested time machine. The families are transported to the Roman Colosseum where Fred and Barney are nearly eaten by lionosauruses. They then travel to Columbus's ship where Wilma discovers America; to King Arthur's Court, where Fred finds himself jousting with a black knight; and to the World's Fair in the twentieth century. After being chased by the police, the couples return to their own epoch, and decide that, although the future is a nice place to visit, they wouldn't want to live there.

MOONLIGHT AND MAINTENANCE

134

Production No.: P-134
Story: Herb Finn/
Alan Dinehart
Recording Date: 7/28/64
Air Date: 1/29/65

Voices:

Alan Reed	Fred, Dinosaur
Mel Blanc	Barney,
	Dino, Elephant
Jean Vander Pyl	Wilma,
	Pebbles,
	Mrs. Wrathrock,
	Old Gal, Mrs. Slate
Gerry Johnson	Betty,
	Woman Tenant,
	Mrs. Rockwell
John Stephenson	Wrathrock,
	Man, Wig Man,
	Slate
Doug Young	Mowersaurus,
	Elevator Monkey,
	Cop, Bird,
	Auto Horn, Joe
Don Messick	Bamm-Bamm,
	Hoppy, Owner,
	Door Monkey,
	Ice Box Monkey,
	Rimrock

Fred decides to move to Bedrock Towers, a new apartment house designed for push-button living. To pay the high rent, Fred assumes the role of resident stationary engineer—building custodian—while keeping his day job at the quarry. The new life is not as easy as it seems, however, since the Flintstone apartment is in the sub-basement and Fred and Wilma are constantly at the mercy of demanding tenants. When the hassle becomes too much, Fred gives up the push-button life to move back to his old neighborhood. Unfortunately, he's leased his house out for a year, so he, Wilma and Pebbles move in with the Rubbles for the remaining 364 days of the term.

SHERIFF FOR A DAY

135

Production No.: P-135
Story: Joanna Lee
Recording Date: 8/10/64
Air Date: 2/5/65

Voices:

Alan Reed	Fred
Mel Blanc	Barney,
	Dino, Bronto
Jean Vander Pyl	Wilma,
	Pebbles
Gerry Johnson	Betty, Kitty
Henry Corden	E. B.,
	Rockeye, Digger,
	Guide, Driver,
	Ben Cartrock
Allan Melvin	Sheriff Crag,
	Slate, Man, Hoss
Don Messick	Bamm-Bamm,
	Hoppy, Barber,
	Announcer, Bird #2
Doug Young	Gas Guy,
	Bird #1, Joe

Out west hunting for uranium, the Flintstones and Rubbles run into an old friend of Fred's named Crag, who is the sheriff of Rocky Gulch. When Fred brags about his gunslinging prowess, Crag makes him sheriff and then disappears, just as the feared Slatery brothers come into town. With Barney as his deputy, Fred gallantly tries to save the town—and himself—from the outlaws. At the eleventh hour, the Cartrocks—prehistoric TV western stars from the Rockerosa ranch—ride in on their dinosaurs to save the day.

DEEP IN THE HEART OF TEXAROCK

136

Production No.: P-136
Story: Barry Blitzer
Recording Date: 8/4/64
Air Date: 2/12/65

Voices:

Alan Reed	Fred
Mel Blanc	Barney,
	Dino,
	Billy the Kidder
Jean Vander Pyl	Wilma,
	Pebbles
Gerry Johnson	Betty, Girl,
	P.A.
Don Messick	Bamm-Bamm,
	Hoppy, Control,
	Clerk, Tortoise,
	Blister
Hal Smith	Dinosaur,
	Pilot, Uncle Tex,
	Cow #1, Hood,
	Carmen
Doug Young	Crab, Elephant, #2
	Hood, Man

The Flintstones and Rubbles fly to Texarock to visit Fred's rich Uncle Tex, whose ranch is so large it has its own ocean. Tex's cowasaurus herd is being raided by Billy the Kidder and his gang. Convincing Fred and Barney to don a cowasaurus skin, Tex instructs the boys to sound the alarm when the rustlers show up. When the thieves arrive, however, Tex fails to hear the signal. The entire herd is stolen, including Fred and Barney. Carmen, a female cowasaurus with a crush on the costumed boys, charges the thieves and sits on them until they are captured. Returning home, the Flintstones and Rubbles receive a reward from Tex—Carmen.

SUPERSTONE

137

Production No.: P-137

Story: Not Available

Recording Date: 8/17/64

Air Date: 2/26/65

Voices:

Alan Reed	Fred
Mel Blanc	Barney, Dino, Boss
Jean Vander Pyl	Wilma, Pebbles
Gerry Johnson	Betty, Girl, Cashier
Allan Melvin	1st Thug, Superstone, Bugsy, Cop, Bartender, Sergeant
Elliot Field	2nd Thug, Manager, Voice, TV Announcer, 3rd Thug
Don Messick	Bamm-Bamm, Hoppy, Exec, Kid, Bird, Paper Boy

When Fred is asked to portray TV hero Superstone (his battle cry: Bee hee hee ha ha) in a promotional appearance, he is knocked unconscious by crooks who don his costume and steal the gate receipts. Soon the police are after Fred—they think he is the thief. Now Fred must save both his reputation and the day. With Barney's help, he follows the thieves to their hide-out, captures them, returns the money to the theater, and becomes a hero himself.

THE ROLLS ROCK CAPER

138

Production No.: P-138

Story: Not Available

Recording Date: 8/28/64

Air Date: 2/19/65

Voices:

Alan Reed	Fred, #3 Thug
Mel Blanc	Barney, Dino, Apartment Thug
Jean Vander Pyl	Wilma, Pebbles, Cookie, Mrs.Mortar, #2, Dame, #1 Dame
Gerry Johnson	Betty, Girl, Waitress, Tootsie, Manicurist, #1 Dame
Don Messick	Bamm-Bamm, Hoppy, Skunk, Fish, #2 Thug, Headwaiter
Allen Melvin	Boulder, Voice, #1 Thug, Pig
Henry Corden	Maitre d', Gus, Ingomar

Fred and Barney are coerced into helping Aaron Boulder, a millionaire cop, solve the murder of a restaurateur. While Boulder chases dames, Fred and Barney try to find the killer and are attacked by every thug in town. Boulder finally zeros in on Mrs. Mortimer Mortar as a prime suspect and sends the boys to pick her up aboard her yacht, which she blows up to avoid capture. When Fred and Barney report back to Boulder, soaking wet from being immersed in the sea, he informs them they've been guests on his new TV show, "Smile, You're on My Favorite Crime."

FRED MEETS HERCUROCK

139

Production No.: P-139

Story: Not Available

Recording Date: 8/31/64

Air Date: 3/5/65

Voices:

Alan Reed	Fred, Duck
Mel Blanc	Barney, Dino, Lizard
Jean Vander Pyl	Wilma, Pebbles, 2nd Girl
Gerry Johnson	Betty, Party Girl, 1st Girl, Lady
Mike Road	Ravine, Guy, Trainer, 2nd Guy, Chauffeur
Don Messick	Bamm-Bamm, Hoppy, Sam, Duck, Crane, Rockhead, 1st Guy

Unfortunate Fred is forced to work on Saturday even though his horoscope says it's his lucky day. Things get better when movie producer Go-Go Ravine casts him as the star of his new picture, *Hercurock and the Maidens*. Fred quits his job at the quarry to get in shape for his movie role. When the film starts rolling, he is charged by a herd of wild elephants and a giant lizard. After a wild chariot race, fed-up Fred quits—leaving Barney to finish the film and kiss the maidens—and takes his quarry job back under the condition that he be allowed to sign autographs for ten cents each during his lunch hour.

SURFIN' FRED

140

Production No.: P-140

Story: Not Available

Recording Date: 9/21/64

Air Date: 3/12/65

Voices:

Alan Reed	Fred
Mel Blanc	Barney, Dino, Manager
Jean Vander Pyl	Wilma, 2nd Girl
Gerry Johnson	Betty, 1st Girl, 3rd Girl
Don Messick	Pelican, 1st Kid, Assistant, Voice, Announcer
James Darren	Jimmy Darrock
Howard Morris	Al, 2nd Boy

Fred takes Wilma and the Rubbles for a quiet weekend at Rock Island, unaware that the National Surfing Finals are being held there at the same time. Just as Fred heads into the surf, the beach is inundated by teens. A big kid himself, Fred becomes a hit with the young crowd, although the lifeguard—teen idol Jimmy Darrock in disguise (voiced by real-life teen idol James Darren)—gets tired of rescuing him from the briny deep. The kids talk Fred into entering the surfing competition, but to prevent a catastrophe, Wilma ends up doing the surfing with Fred on her shoulders. Hanging ten like pros, they shoot the pier and win first prize.

THE HOUSE THAT FRED BUILT

141

Production No.: P-141
Story: Joanna Lee
Recording Date: 3/2/65
Air Date: 9/24/65

Voices:

Jean Vander Pyl	Wilma, Pebbles
Gerry Johnson	Betty
Don Messick	Bamm-Bamm, Monkey, Announcer, Bird
Sam Edwards	Mailman, Agent, Marv
Alan Reed	Fred
Mel Blanc	Barney, Dino, Alex
Janet Waldo	Mrs. Slaghoople

When Wilma receives a letter from her mother saying she's going to move in with her favorite son-in-law, Fred buys a dilapidated house in a deserted development called Stony Acres. He and Barney spend every evening fixing it into a cozy haven for Mrs. Slaghoople. Their wives, suspecting they're seeing other women, follow and arrive just as the little house is completed. Wilma is delighted—until the house, built over a well, fills with water, slides off its foundation, and crashes over a cliff. The next morning Mrs. Slaghoople arrives on her motorcycle and informs them that the son-in-law she's going to stay with is Wilma's sister's husband, not Fred.

NO BIZ LIKE SHOW BIZ

142

Production No.: P-142
Story: Joanna Lee
Recording Date: 4/13/65
Air Date: 9/17/65

Voices:

Alan Reed	Fred
Mel Blanc	Barney, Dino, Driver
Jean Vander Pyl	Wilma, Pebbles, 1st Girl
Gerry Johnson	Betty, 2nd Girl
Don Messick	Bamm-Bamm, Announcer, Disk Jockey, 1st Boy, Photographer, 1st Cop, Attendant, Doctor
Bernard Fox	Eppy Brianstone

Wakened from a nap by the sound of music, Fred goes into the yard to discover that Pebbles and Bamm-Bamm are singing. Teenage impresario Eppy Brianstone, whose car has broken down outside the Flintstone home, hears the kids in song and signs on as their manager. They become a smashing success and hit the road on tour, accompanied by Wilma and Betty. Suffering from loneliness, Fred and Barney don disguises and kidnap the tiny singing sensations. A wild chase ensues and just as the police close in, Fred wakes up and realizes he has dreamed the whole thing.

DISORDER IN THE COURT

143

Production No.: P-143
Story: Herb Finn/ Alan Dinehart
Recording Date: 4/23/65
Air Date: 10/8/65

Voices:

Alan Reed	Fred
Mel Blanc	Barney, Dino, Judge
Jean Vander Pyl	Wilma, Pebbles, Mother Quartzstone
Gerry Johnson	Betty, Phone Operator
Don Messick	Bamm-Bamm, Hoppy, Bird, 1st Juryman, Arnold, Brush, Radio, Cop
Henry Corden	Mangler, 2nd Juryman, Chief
Daws Butler	Defense Attorney, Bailiff, Shale

When Fred and Barney are summoned to serve on a jury, Fred ends up as the foreman. The case, the trial of Mangler, turns ugly when Mangler is sentenced to prison and vows to get Fred if it takes him the rest of his life. Before long, Mangler escapes from jail and comes looking for Fred. The Flintstones and Rubbles hide out at Barney's cabin on Echo Rock Lake, protected—although they don't know it—by police detective Shale. Fred and Barney mistake Shale for the Mangler, throw a tablecloth over his head and lock him in a closet, just as the real Mangler arrives. The big brute gains entry to the cabin, slips on Bamm-Bamm's toy train, and is recaptured.

THE RETURN OF STONY CURTIS

144

Production No.: P-144
Story: Harvey Bullock/ R. Allen
Recording Date: 6/21/65
Air Date: 10/1/65

Voices:

Alan Reed	Fred
Mel Blanc	Barney, Bird, Dinosaur
Jean Vander Pyl	Wilma, 2nd Woman
Gerry Johnson	Betty, 1st Woman, Jennifer, Mabel
John Stephenson	Cop, Mr. Slate, Actor #1, Actor #3
Tony Curtis	Stony
Don Messick	Rocco, Actor #2, Willie

Movie star Stony Curtis—voiced by real-life star Tony Curtis—comes to Bedrock to film his new flick, *Slave Boy*. Wilma wins a promotional contest in which the prize is Stony as her slave for a day, but when she can't be reached, Stony is awarded to Fred. Determined to prove the movie star is not a real he-man, Fred forces his "slave" to perform manual labor. To stop this, Stony tells Fred he's got acting ability and arranges for him to be his stand-in in the movie. Fred promptly quits his job and puts his house on the market, but when he learns Stony's cushy job involves fighting alligators, he renounces his new career. When the buyer of Fred's house arrives, Stony—pretending to be an amorous next-door neighbor—flirts with the man's wife so that he backs out of the deal.

THE GREAT GAZOO

145

Production No.: P-145

Story: Joanna Lee

Recording Date: 6/17/65

Air Date: 10/29/65

Voices:

Alan Reed	Fred
Mel Blanc	Barney, Dino
Jean Vander Pyl	Wilma,
	Pebbles
Gerry Johnson	Betty
Harvey Korman	Gazoo,
	Cop, Maitre d', Don
Don Messick	Bamm-Bamm

Fred and Barney rescue tiny green Gazoo of the planet Zetox from his flying saucer/time capsule. The snooty little traveler tells them he's been sent into exile on Earth as punishment for inventing a device that has the power to disintegrate the universe. His sentence: faithfully serve his rescuers. Later, thinking that Gazoo will foot the bill, Fred and Barney take their wives to a lavish dinner at the expensive Chateau Rockinbleu. When the check arrives, the little man is nowhere to be found and the Flintstones and Rubbles end up washing dishes to pay for their meals. Finally Gazoo appears, explaining that he had fallen asleep by accident.

CIRCUS BUSINESS

146

Production No.: P-146

Story: Herb Finn/

Alan Dinehart

Recording Date: 6/10/65

Air Date: 10/15/65

Voices:

Alan Reed	Fred, Turtle
Mel Blanc	Barney,
	Dino, Clipper Bird,
	Rollem, Circus Bird
Jean Vander Pyl	Wilma,
	Pebbles, Fat Lady
Gerry Johnson	Betty, Mrs.
	Rollem, Madam,
	Half Woman
Allen Melvin	Mailman, 1st Head,
	Tom, Thin Man,
	Prospector
Hal Smith	Lawn Mower,
	2nd Head, Rocky,
	Rover, Kid, Gummo
Henry Corden	Dick,
	Attendant, Barker,
	Half Man,
	Sherrif, Herculo
Don Messick	Bamm-Bamm

With his income tax refund of thirty-seven dollars, Fred takes his family and the Rubbles to the circus. Unaware that the unpaid performers are about to quit, he purchases the place from the owner, Rollem. When Fred can't pay the performers either, they walk away, and the sheriff threatens to imprison Fred for misrepresentation if the show does not go on. Left with little choice, Fred, Barney, Dino, and Hoppy perform all the acts—Barney is the human cannonball, Dino and Hoppy box, and Fred does a high-wire act and dives four hundred feet into a pail of water. Seeing that the show is successful, the performers return and Rollem buys back the circus.

RIP VAN FLINTSTONE

147

Production No.: P-147

Story: Tony Benedict

Recording Date: 6/15/65

Air Date: 11/5/65

Voices:

Alan Reed	Fred
Mel Blanc	Barney,
	Dino, Kid, Fang
Jean Vander Pyl	Wilma,
	Pebbles
Gerry Johnson	Betty,
	Lady, Woman
Daws Butler	Clerk, Sandy,
	2nd Guy,
	2nd Player, Butler
John Stephenson	Slate,
	Guard
Henry Corden	1st Guy,
	3rd Guy, Hunter,
	Player, Neighbor,
	Bamm-Bamm Grown-Up
Don Messick	Bamm-Bamm

Disdaining the games at the Slate Construction Annual Picnic, Fred climbs a hill and falls asleep. He wakes up with white hair and a long white beard to discover that the town has grown. Barney is now multi-millionaire B. J. Rubble, Pebbles and Bamm-Bamm have gotten married, and Wilma has grown old. Awakening from this dream, Fred finds his wife still young and beautiful, and is so jubilant that he races down the hill, joins in the games, and wins every event, including a trophy for Inspirational Employee of the Year.

SAMANTHA

148

Production No.: P-148

Story: Harvey Bullock/

R. Allen

Recording Date: 6/24/65

Air Date: 10/22/65

Voices:

Alan Reed	Fred
Mel Blanc	Barney, Dino,
	Bird, Lew, Lizard,
	Brontosaurus,
	Tyglon, Kitten
Jean Vander Pyl	Wilma,
	Pebbles
Gerry Johnson	Betty
Don Messick	Bamm-Bamm,
	Paul, Octopus
Elizabeth Montgomery	Samantha
Dick York	Darrin

Convincing Wilma and Betty that women are unfit for the rigors of life in the woods, Fred and Barney leave for a weekend of fishing and hunting by themselves. At the same time, Samantha and Darrin of "Bewitched" fame—voiced by the show's actors Elizabeth Montgomery and Dick York—move in across the street. When Darrin leaves for a weekend of boating, Samantha takes Wilma and Betty into the woods to prove that girls are as tough as guys. With the help of her magic, the girls outmaneuver Fred and Barney in everything from raising tents to fishing for food. However, when the boys suggest that they arise at dawn, climb a mountain while carrying canoes, and go for an icy swim, the girls decide to go home.

THE GRAVELBERRY PIE KING

149

Production No.: P-149

Story: Herb Finn/
Alan Dinehart

Recording Date: 7/1/65

Air Date: 11/12/65

Voices:

Alan Reed	Fred
Mel Blanc	Barney, Dino, Harry
Jean Vander Pyl	Wilma, Pebbles
Gerry Johnson	Betty
John Stephenson	Slate, Hilary, Chauffeur
Harvey Korman	Gazoo, Safestone, Buddy, Officer
Hal Smith	Time Card Animal, Dick, Photographer, Bird, Whistle Bird

Fred presents Mr. Slate with his fellow workers' demands for a pay raise. Slate fires him. Determined to withhold the bad news from Wilma, Fred goes to the park the next morning where he meets supermarket tycoon Mr. Safestone. The tycoon becomes enamored of the gravelberry pie Wilma baked for her husband's lunch and gives Fred an order for fifty pies—with an order of five hundred more upon delivery. To fill this order, all the Flintstones and Rubbles pitch in to bake. When Wilma tells Fred the pies he's been selling for forty cents each cost fifty-two cents apiece to make, he raises the price—but he makes it so high that Safestone cancels the order. Fred and Barney then try to sell the pies to passing motorists but are stopped by a policeman who demands to see their license. Wilma takes over and sells the recipe to Safestone—becoming the Gravelberry Pie Queen—and persuades Slate to rehire Fred.

THE STONEFINGER CAPER

150

Production No.: P-150

Story: Joanna Lee

Recording Date: 7/8/65

Air Date: 11/19/65

Voices:

Alan Reed	Fred
Mel Blanc	Barney, Lew, Bird
Jean Vander Pyl	Wilma, Pebbles, Tiny Horrasaurus
Gerry Johnson	Betty
Henry Corden	Crusher, Pond, Cop, Don Horrorasaurus, Paul
Harvey Korman	Gazoo, Stonefinger

The evil Stonefinger orders his men to kidnap Dr. Rockenheimer, the man who discovered how to turn stone into uraniumrock—and who looks just like Barney. Meanwhile Gazoo conjures up a fancy Maserocki sport scar for Fred and Barney. While driving in the new car, Barney is spotted by Stonefinger's men, who believe he's Rockenheimer. The thugs capture the boys and threaten to feed Barney to a hungry horrorasaurus if he doesn't produce the formula. Gazoo comes to the rescue and turns Stonefinger and his men into babies.

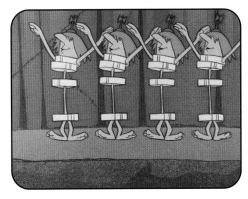

THE MASQUERADE PARTY

151

Production No.: P-151

Story: Warren Foster

Recording Date: 7/15/65

Air Date: 11/26/65

Voices:

Alan Reed	Fred, 1st Guy, 2nd Crowd
Mel Blanc	Barney, Dino, Bird, Boss
Jean Vander Pyl	Wilma, Pebbles, Dame #1, Dame #2, 1st Voice
Gerry Johnson	Betty, 3rd Voice, Jill, Girl
John Stephenson	Grand Poobah, Sergeant, 2nd Man, 2nd Voice, 3rd Way-Out, 3rd Crowd
Allen Melvin	Sam, Cop #2, Beast, Leader, 1st Man, Cabbie, Chef, 2nd Guy, 2nd Way-Out, Sports Announcer, Guard, 1st Crowd
Don Messick	Bamm-Bamm, Eddie, Jack, 1st Way-Out, Cop #1, Man, Bee, Scoop, 4th Way-Out
Janet Waldo	Janie, Woman

The Water Buffalos hold a costume party and Fred, who has won for originality five years in a row, is confident of winning again. Meanwhile, the local radio station signs up the Wayouts, a singing foursome. In a publicity stunt, the group's PR man announces that the Wayouts are creatures from another planet and are loose in the streets. Fred, in a space suit costume, is caught up in the panic. No one believes that he is not an alien, and the Water Buffalos throw him out when he arrives at the party with the music group. When the hoax is revealed, the Water Buffalos apologize to Fred and once again award him first prize for his costume.

SHINROCK-A-GO-GO

152

Production No.: P-152

Story: Barry Blitzer

Recording Date: 7/22/65

Air Date: 12/3/65

Voices:

Alan Reed	Fred
Mel Blanc	Barney, Dino, General
Jean Vander Pyl	Wilma, Pebbles
Gerry Johnson	Betty, Gal, Secretary, 2nd Pterodactyl
Don Messick	Bamm-Bamm, Hoppy, TV Announcer, Chimp, Scrub Bird, Doorman, 1st Pterodactyl, Voice, Disk Jockey
Allen Melvin	Voices, Arthur, Newscaster, McShale, Teenager, 1st Boy
Jimmy O'Neill	Jimmy O'Neillstone

Shinrock, a dance show, is Betty and Wilma's favorite TV program. When Jimmy O'Neillstone, the emcee—voiced by real "Shindig" host Jimmy O'Neill—invites the viewing audience to the studio, they plan to go with the boys. At the bowling alley before the show, Fred drops a ball on his foot. When it is reinjured at the TV station, and he begins to howl and jump, Jimmy is sure it's a new dance. Naming it The Frantic, he hires Fred to introduce it on the air. Just before going on, Fred sits on a pin and hollers and jumps anew, which leads Jimmy to believe he's created yet another new dance, the Flintstone Flop. Realizing that every time Fred gets hurt, he makes up a new dance, Barney says Fred will make a fortune, if he lives.

ROYAL RUBBLE

153

Production No.: P-153

Story: Tony Benedict

Recording Date: 7/27/65

Air Date: 12/10/65

Voices:

Alan Reed	Fred
Mel Blanc	Barney, Dino, Clerk
Jean Vander Pyl	Wilma,
	Pebbles,
	Roberta, Girl
Gerry Johnson	Betty,
	Guyla, Girl
Don Messick	Bamm-Bamm, Harry,
	Animal, Turtle, Guy
Harvey Korman	Don, Bird,
	Heir, Bill
Allen Melvin	Paul, Joe,
	Bellhop, Guard

Two turbaned men tell Barney he's long-lost Prince Barbaruba of Stony-rock-arabia and escort him to the Rocktop Plaza Hotel to receive lessons in diction, dancing, and country-running before his coronation on the following day. Although Wilma and Betty are thrilled by Barney's good fortune, Fred is suspicious and believes he might actually be kidnapped. Hurrying to the hotel on a rescue mission, Fred finds his pal happily going along with the coronation plans. When the boys fail to return, Wilma and Betty also head for the hotel and are thrown in with two hundred girls who have come to apply for Barney's harem. When the wives leave in a snit, and Barney tries to abdicate, he's threatened with death and is only released when the real heir to the throne is found.

SEEING DOUBLES

154

Production No.: P-154

Story: George O'Hanlon

Recording Date: 8/3/65

Air Date: 12/17/65

Voices:

Alan Reed	Fred
Mel Blanc	Barney,
	Dino, Rabbit
Jean Vander Pyl	Wilma,
	Pebbles, Mrs. Slate
Gerry Johnson	Betty
John Stephenson	Truck Driver,
	Cop, Slate,
	Cab Driver
Don Messick	Announcer,
	Teammate, Waiter
Harvey Korman	Gazoo

Fred and Barney try to get out of taking their wives to dinner on the night they're scheduled to bowl in a play-off game. Gazoo creates doubles for the boys, who take Wilma and Betty out to dinner while the real Fred and Barney drive off to the bowling tournament. The doubles are capable only of saying, "Yes, yes, yes," and "no, no, no," but the girls are delighted when they are taken to an expensive restaurant. Fearing trouble, Fred and Barney try to remove their look-alikes, but Mr. Slate bumps into them and soon the doubles are dancing with Mrs. Slate while the real Fred and Barney dance with Betty and Wilma. The boys dump bowls of soup on the doubles and put them in the car, but the doubles drive away, leaving Fred and Barney stranded on the road. Back at home, the boys lure their doubles outside, and finally succeed in having them banished by Gazoo.

HOW TO PICK A FIGHT WITH YOUR WIFE WITHOUT REALLY TRYING

155

Production No.: P-155

Story: Herb Finn/

Alan Dinehart

Recording Date: 8/4/65

Air Date: 1/7/66

Voices:

Alan Reed	Fred
Mel Blanc	Barney, Dino, Turtle
Jean Vander Pyl	Wilma,
	Pebbles, Mrs. Bunny
Gerry Johnson	Betty,
	Cuckoo, Clerk
Don Messick	Elephant, Bronto,
	Bird, Cuckoo
Harvey Korman	Gazoo, Mr.
	Bunny, Man

Gazoo tells Fred that men have superior minds and should treat women like children. Meanwhile, Betty tells Wilma that women have superior minds and should treat their husbands like children. With the tension mounting, Fred buys a Rockopoly game, hoping it will calm things down. When the two couples play, the Flintstones end up in a fight and Fred leaves home to live with Barney while Betty stays with Wilma. Betty and Barney try to make the best of the situation while Fred and Wilma try to prove they don't need each other. That night, Wilma dreams that she's being carried off by an Arabian prince; Fred dreams Wilma is a Rockette. They then wake up and rush into each other's arms.

TWO MEN ON A DINOSAUR

156

Production No.: P-156

Story: Walter Black

Recording Date: 8/17/65

Air Date: 2/4/66

Voices:

Alan Reed	Fred
Mel Blanc	Barney
Jean Vander Pyl	Wilma,
	Pebbles
Gerry Johnson	Betty
Harvey Korman	Gazoo,
	Gazaam
Don Messick	Bamm-Bamm,
	Hoppy, Cop,
	Announcer,
	Needle Nose, Voice
Henry Corden	Paul,
	Stony, Ed

Poor Gazoo has a bad day—first Gazaam, his superior on Planet Zetox, refuses to allow him to return home. Then Fred and Barney refuse to accept his tips on the dinosaur races. When his choices win, however, they change their minds and soon parlay four dollars into two hundred. A couple of bookies decide the boys have a great system and force Fred and Barney to accompany them to their boss, Big Ed. Big Ed insists the boys name the winners at Boulder Downs, so Gazoo—who has followed—imparts the names of three losers. When Big Ed and his men return to beat up Fred and Barney, Gazoo magically makes them beat up themselves. "If you can't afford to lose, you can't afford to win," the little spaceman lectures his two charges, who agree.

FRED GOES APE

157

Production No.: P-157
Story: Barry Blitzer
Recording Date: 8/5/65
Air Date: 1/14/66

Voices:

Alan Reed	Fred
Mel Blanc	Barney, Dino, Vulture, Annie
Jean Vander Pyl	Wilma, Pebbles, Mrs. Boulderdame, 1st Old Maid
Gerry Johnson	Betty, TV Girl, 2nd Old Maid
Don Messick	Announcer, Fred as Ape, TV Voice, Goosepimple, Waiter, Cop, 1st Guy, Guard

Tired of sneezing all the time, Fred goes to the pharmacy with Barney to buy a bottle of Scram pills. He gets hold of Goosepimple's Pepstone Pills instead, and turns into an ape when he takes one. Barney returns home to break the news to Wilma, but the effects of the pill wear off and Fred returns to his normal self. The next day, the families go to the zoo, where Fred takes another pill and once again becomes simian. The guards put him in the ape cage, and when the medication wears off, he is unable to explain how he got inside. When Barney begins sneezing, Fred gives him the last of his pills and Barney becomes an ape.

THE LONG, LONG, LONG WEEKEND

158

Production No.: P-158
Story: Herb Finn/ Alan Dinehart
Recording Date: 8/19/65
Air Date: 1/21/66

Voices:

Alan Reed	Fred, Passenger
Mel Blanc	Barney, Dino, Duck
Jean Vander Pyl	Wilma, Pebbles
Gerry Johnson	Betty, Lady
John Stephenson	Slate, Doorman, Drive #1, Barber, Monster Actor, Director
Don Messick	Bamm-Bamm, Dinosaur, Dad, Mechanical Voice, Waiter, Rocket Driver, Creature, 2nd Creature, Boy
Janet Waldo	Girl, Stewardess, Mother
Harvey Korman	Gazoo

Fred asks Mr. Slate for a four-dollar advance on his salary and the boss agrees with the proviso that Fred pay six percent interest and take out life insurance. Later, Fred finds Barney reading a magazine about life in the twenty-first century and calls it junk. Gazoo decides to show the Flintstones and Rubbles the future first-hand. The Flintmobile is magically transformed into a flying saucer, and the two couples tour futuristic Bedrock. At the Slate Rock and Gravel Company, Fred bumps into Mr. Slate the 80,000th and discovers the interest on his loan amounts to over 23 million dollars. The Flintstones and Rubbles return to their own time, and Fred vows to repay the four dollars immediately.

THE TREASURE OF THE SIERRA MADROCK

159

Production No.: P-159
Story: Joanna Lee
Recording Date: 8/20/65
Air Date: 2/11/66

Voices:

Alan Reed	Fred
Mel Blanc	Barney, Zeke, Evil Eye
Jean Vander Pyl	Wilma, Pebbles
Gerry Johnson	Betty
Henry Corden	Zack, 1st Villain, 1st Buzzard, Turtle
Don Messick	Bamm-Bamm, 2nd Villain, 2nd Buzzard, Bird, Pelican, Donkey

Returning from a vacation in Rock Vegas, the Flintstones and Rubbles meet Zack and Zeke, two con artists posing as gold diggers, who trick the boys into thinking they're in the richest gold territory in the country. Although Wilma and Betty find evidence that their husbands are being conned, they keep silent until they learn the boys have paid real money for a land claim. Then Zack and Zeke find evidence—planted by the girls—that the boys have found treasure. When Fred and Barney refuse to sell back the claim, Zack and Zeke try to do away with them. After they send them over a cliff into a raging river, Fred throws away the claim—which is immediately grabbed by a couple of other criminals who have been following the families the whole time—and the Flintstones and Rubbles return home.

CURTAIN CALL AT BEDROCK

160

Production No.: P-160
Story: George O'Hanlon
Recording Date: 9/7/65
Air Date: 2/18/66

Voices:

Alan Reed	Fred
Mel Blanc	Barney, Dino, Traffic Signal
Jean Vander Pyl	Wilma, Pebbles, Girl
Gerry Johnson	Betty
Don Messick	Hoppy, Worker, Mastodon, Henry
John Stephenson	Rockhead, Foreman, Steam Shovel, Charlie
Harvey Korman	Gazoo

When Wilma is put in charge of the PTA show "Romeorock and Julietstone," she casts herself as the female lead and Fred as Romeorock. When Fred turns down the part, Barney is cast as the lovesick lead. Fred coaches his pal, but even with Gazoo's help, he is unable to make Barney play the part with feeling. On opening night, Barney fakes the mumps and Fred takes over. But when an attack of laryngitis cuts short Wilma's version of Julietstone, Barney takes her place. The boys turn tragedy into success, with newspapers predicting the show will be a smash on Broadrockaway.

BOSS FOR A DAY

161

Production No.: P-161
Story: Walter Black
Recording Date: 9/13/65
Air Date: 2/25/66

Voices:

Alan Reed	Fred
Mel Blanc	Barney, Dino, President
Jean Vander Pyl	Wilma, Pebbles
Gerry Johnson	Betty, Miss Slag
Don Messick	Bamm-Bamm, 1st Bird, Parrot, Elephant, Dinosaur, #1 Man, Board Member #1, Board Member #3
John Stephenson	English Chauffeur, #2 Man, Slate
Allen Melvin	Mac, Foreman, Accountant, #2 Board Member
Harvey Korman	Gazoo

After a tough day at the quarry in which everyone, especially Mr. Slate, has given him a hard time, Fred tells Gazoo he'd like to be in charge just once. Gazoo promises him he'll be the boss the next day. In the morning, a chauffeured limousine takes Fred to work, where he proceeds to throw his weight around. Then the chairman of the board puts him in his place by letting him know who's really the boss. Suddenly, Fred has more woes than he ever imagined. Happy when the regular workday is over, he finds that that's when the boss must really go to work, especially if the chairman is around. When Fred's day finally ends, he decides he wouldn't be in Slate's shoes for anything and thanks Gazoo for the lesson.

FRED'S ISLAND

162

Production No.: P-162
Story: Barry Blitzer
Recording Date: 9/14/65
Air Date: 3/4/66

Voices:

Alan Reed	Fred, Rhino
Mel Blanc	Barney, Dino
Jean Vander Pyl	Wilma, Pebbles, Doris, Mrs. Slate, 2nd Wife
Gerry Johnson	Betty, Lady, Panicky Gal, Wife, 3rd Wife
Don Messick	Bamm-Bamm, Hoppy, Dinosaur, Commodore, Brat, Bosun Bird, Serpent, Guide, Man
John Stephenson	Foreman, Slate
Henry Corden	Savage, Ape

Mr. Slate invites the Flintstones to spend the day on his yacht, the S.S. *Mogulrock*, while he and his wife visit Bedrockland, a new amusement park. The catch is that they must paint the vessel while aboard. Fred invites the Rubbles to come along—so Barney can help with the painting. Before long, the yacht breaks away and drifts to an island which they believe is deserted. While on the island, Fred and Barney meet a savage they name Saturday and discover a volcano. Later they learn the island is really a part of Bedrockland; Slate discovers Fred and charges him with larceny, mutiny, and piracy. But when the volcano erupts, Fred becomes a hero when he uses the yacht to rescue everyone.

JEALOUSY

163

Production No.: P-163
Story: Harvey Bullock/ R. Allen
Recording Date: 9/24/65
Air Date: 3/11/66

Voices:

Alan Reed	Fred
Mel Blanc	Barney, Bird, Turtle
Jean Vander Pyl	Wilma, Woman #2
Gerry Johnson	Woman #1, Woman #3
Don Messick	Wilbur, Octopus, Bowler, #1 Man, #2 Man
Harvey Korman	Gazoo

Once again Fred finds himself in trouble when the Lodge bowling tournament coincides with a violin recital he has promised to attend with Wilma. Feigning a headache, he agrees to let her go with her old school chum, Wilbur Terwilligerock. When Wilbur comes to pick Wilma up, Fred discovers that the man is tall and handsome, an Olymprock athlete, a wonderful pianist, and driver of a brand new Rockarrari sports car. After Wilma and her escort drive away, Fred and Barney go to the bowling alley, but poor Fred's mind is not on the game and they depart for the restaurant where they find Wilma and Wilbur dancing. Gazoo turns Barney into Fred's date, Barbara, in hopes of making Wilma jealous, but it doesn't work. Chastened, Fred tells Gazoo that if he had it to do over, he'd never lie to Wilma again. At home, Wilma admits she found Wilbur a bore. Fred confesses to lying, but when he adds that she should never have left him alone, Gazoo hits him in the face with a rockleberry pie.

DRIPPER

164

Production No.: P-164
Story: Barry Blitzer
Recording Date: 10/1/65
Air Date: 3/18/66

Voices:

Alan Reed	Fred
Mel Blanc	Barney, Swordfish
Jean Vander Pyl	Wilma, Pebbles, Mrs. Big
Gerry Johnson	Betty, Cashier, Mermaid
Don Messick	Announcer, 2nd Driver, 4th Driver, Reporter, Blinky, Dripper, Keystone, Announcer
Henry Corden	1st Driver, 3rd Driver, Muscles, Trainer, Police Sergeant, Cop
Doug Young	Copter Bird, Octopus, Chief

The Flintstones and Rubbles take a Sunday outing to the Oceanrock Aquarium to see Dripper, the performing sealosaurus. Muscles and Blinky—who is acutely myopic—are also at the aquarium, planning to kidnap the animal on the orders of their boss, Mrs. Big. Dripper takes a liking to Barney and follows him to his car after the show. When the Flintstones and Rubbles arrive home and take a dip in the pool, they discover the sealosaurus, but not Muscles and Blinky, who have trailed them. Near-sighted Blinky mistakes Barney for Dripper, shoves him into the sack, and takes him to Mrs. Big. Dripper follows and alerts the police. The thieves are arrested and Mrs. Big is revealed as Dripper's trainer, who was jealous of the animal's fame.

THE STORY OF ROCKY'S RAIDERS

165

Production No.: P-165

Story: Joanna Lee

Recording Date: 10/5/65

Air Date: 4/1/66

Voices:

Jean Vander Pyl	Wilma, Pebbles, Mata
Alan Reed	Fred, Rocky, Grandpa
Mel Blanc	Barney, Reggie
Gerry Johnson	Betty, Fifi
Don Messick	Bamm-Bamm, Man, 1st Pilot, 1st German Soldier, 3rd German Soldier
Henry Corden	Rickenrock, 2nd Pilot, 2nd German Soldier

With Grandpa Flintstone's imminent arrival, the Flintstones and Rubbles read his World War I diary and flash back to his exploits as Lt. Rocky Flintstone (Fred) and his buddy, Lt. Reggie Vanderock (Barney). Leaving Fifi, a French resistance worker (Betty with brown hair and a beauty mark), Rocky and Reggie set off to rescue Mata Harock (Wilma), the world's most famous spy, who is being held prisoner behind enemy lines. After a thrilling dogfight with Baron Von Rickenrock, they rescue Mata, and the trio escapes on a bicycle, pursued by the Baron. Trapped, they manage to pick off all their foes except Von Rickenrock. Here the diary ends and the Flintstones and Rubbles reluctantly return to the present. Grandpa Flintstone arrives with Reggie, tailed by Von Rickenrock—who's been chasing them for over half a century—in his bi-plane.

MY FAIR FREDDY

166

Production No.: P-166

Story: Tony Benedict

Recording Date: 10/20/65

Air Date: 3/25/66

Voices:

Alan Reed	Fred, Elephant, 5th Guy
Mel Blanc	Barney, Bird, 2nd Guy
Jean Vander Pyl	Wilma, Pebbles, Adell
Gerry Johnson	Betty, Sophia, Olive, Wife
Harvey Korman	Narrator, Stevens, Gazoo
Henry Corden	Rockhead, 4th Guy, Man
Don Messick	Bamm-Bamm, Cop, 1st Guy, 3rd Guy

When Fred applies for membership at the swank Stonyside Country Club, the members decide to check on the Flintstones' background. They arrive just as Wilma is telling Betty that Dino has received papers indicating he's a descendant of a royal dinosaur family, and think she's referring to Fred. They immediately approve his membership, but Wilma worries whether they'll fit in with the society crowd. Gazoo offers to teach Fred culture and soon has him performing a ballet routine. When the Lodge brothers rib Fred about his ballet costume, he decides that he and Wilma will just be themselves at the club ball.

INDEX

PICTURE CREDITS

Page 4: Phillip Brooker; page 5: Phillip Brooker; page 6: Phillip Brooker; page 7: Phillip Brooker; page 8: Phillip Brooker; page 9: Phillip Brooker; page 10: Phillip Brooker; page 11: Phillip Brooker; page 12: Phillip Brooker; page 13: Hanna-Barbera; page 16: Phillip Brooker; pages 18–19: from the collection of Justin Strauss, photography by Nora Scarlett; page 20: Michael Langelo/Archive Photos; page 22: top, Dick Bickenbach; middle, Ed Benedict; bottom, Ed Benedict; page 23: all Ed Benedict; page 24: top, Russell Levin; bottom, Ed Benedict; page 25: all Ed Benedict; page 26: all Ed Benedict; page 27: Ed Benedict; page 28: Hanna-Barbera; page 29: top, Hanna-Barbera; bottom, Ed Benedict; page 30: top, Ed Benedict; middle, Jordan Reicheck; bottom, Jordan Reicheck; page 31: Jordan Reicheck; page 32: all Hanna-Barbera; page 34: top, Ed Benedict; bottom, Hanna-Barbera; page 35: top, Carlos Chavez; bottom, Hanna-Barbera; page 36: all Ed Benedict; page 37: top, Dick Bickenbach; middle, Jerry Eisenberg; bottom, Tony Benedict; page 38: Hanna-Barbera; page 39: all Hanna-Barbera; page 40: Tony Benedict/Tonytoons; page 42: Turner Entertainment Co.; page 43: Tony Benedict/Tonytoons; page 44: Hanna-Barbera; page 45: Turner Entertainment Co.; page 46: top, Hanna-Barbera; bottom, Dick Bickenbach; page 47: Turner Entertainment Co.; pages 48–49: Hanna-Barbera; page 50: all Turner Entertainment Co.; page 51: Tony Benedict/Tonytoons; page 52: top, Dick Bickenbach; bottom, Hanna-Barbera; page 53: Hanna-Barbera; page 54: Jerry Eisenberg; page 56: top, Jerry Eisenberg; middle, Hanna-Barbera; bottom, Hanna-Barbera; page 57: Ed Benedict; page 58: top, Hanna-Barbera; bottom, Tony Benedict/Tonytoons; page 59: all Hanna-Barbera; page 60: all Jerry Eisenberg; page 61: Hanna-Barbera; page 62: Hanna-Barbera; page 63: top, Hanna-Barbera; bottom, Jordan Reicheck; page 64: Hoyt Curtin/photo by Colorhouse; page 65: all Hanna-Barbera; page 66: all Jerry Eisenberg; page 67: all Hanna-Barbera; pages 68 and 69: from the collection of Justin Strauss, photography by Nora Scarlett; page 70: Preston Blair; page 72: Ed Benedict; page 73: courtesy Viewmaster; page 74: Hanna-Barbera; page 75: all Hanna-Barbera; page 76: Hanna-Barbera; page 77: Capital Cities/ABC Inc.; page 78: top left, Hanna-Barbera; top middle, Capital Cities/ABC Inc.; top right, Capital Cities/ABC Inc.; bottom left, Hanna-Barbera; bottom right, Hanna-Barbera; page 79: top, Hanna-Barbera; middle, Preston Blair; bottom, Hanna-Barbera; page 80: Hanna-Barbera; pages 80 and 81: Hanna-Barbera; pages 82 and 83: Hanna-Barbera; page 84: Capital Cities/ABC Inc.; page 85: Hanna-Barbera; page 86: top left, Preston Blair; top middle, Hanna-Barbera; top right, Jean Vander Pyl; middle left, Jordan Reicheck; middle right, Capital Cities/ABC Inc.; bottom left, Hanna-Barbera; page 87: left, Capital Cities/ABC Inc.; top, Hanna-Barbera; middle, Jordan Reicheck; bottom, Hanna-Barbera; page 88: Capital Cities/ABC Inc.; pages 88–89: Capital Cities/ABC Inc.; page 90: Captial Cities/ABC Inc.; page 91: all, Hanna-Barbera; page 92: top left, Jordan Reicheck; middle left, Hanna-Barbera; right, Capital Cities/ABC Inc.; page 93: top, Capital Cities/ABC Inc.; middle left, Hanna-Barbera; middle center, Jordan Reicheck; middle right, Jordan Reicheck; bottom left, Ed Benedict; bottom center, Jordan Reicheck; bottom right, Jordan Reicheck; page 94: Capital Cities/ABC Inc.; page 95: Capital Cities/ABC Inc.; page 96: top, Capital Cities/ABC Inc.; top middle, Hanna-Barbera; center middle, Hanna-Barbera; bottom middle, Hanna-Barbera; bottom, Preston Blair; page 97: top left, Jean Vander Pyl; middle, Hanna-Barbera; bottom ABC; right, Preston Blair; page 98: Scott Maiko; page 99: top left, Capital Cities/ABC Inc.; top right, Capital Cities/ABC Inc.; middle right, Capital Cities/ABC Inc.; bottom, Capital Cities/ABC Inc.; pages 100–101: Hanna-Barbera; page 101: Hanna-Barbera; page 102: top, Hanna-Barbera; bottom, Capital Cities/ABC Inc.; page 103: top, Hanna-Barbera; middle, Hanna-Barbera; bottom, Capital Cities/ABC Inc.; page 104: left, Hanna-Barbera; middle, Capital Cities/ABC Inc.; right, Captial Cities/ABC Inc.; page 105: all Capital Cities/ABC Inc.; page 106: Hanna-Barbera; page 107: Hanna-Barbera; page 108: Hanna-Barbera; page 109: all Hanna-Barbera; pages 110–11: from the collection of Justin Strauss, photography by Nora Scarlett; page 112: Ed Benedict; page 114: top, Hanna-Barbera; bottom, Hanna-Barbera; page 115: top, Hanna-Barbera; bottom, Hanna-Barbera; pages 116 and 117: all Hanna-Barbera; page 118: top and bottom, Hanna-Barbera; page 119: top, Jerry Eisenberg; bottom left, Preston Blair; bottom right, Hanna-Barbera; page 120: all Universal City Studios & Amblin Entertainment; page 121: Hanna-Barbera; page 122: all Hanna-Barbera; page 123: Capital Cities/ABC Inc.; page 124: from the collection of Justin Strauss, photography by Nora Scarlett; page 126: top left and right from the collection of Justin Strauss, photography by Nora Scarlett; middle left and right, Hanna-Barbera; bottom, Jordan Reicheck; page 127: top left, Jeff Eckert; top right, Chronicle Features; middle left, Chronicle Features; middle right, Los Angeles Times Syndicate; bottom right and left from the collection of Justin Strauss, photography by Nora Scarlett; page 128: top, Preston Blair; bottom, Hanna-Barbera; top, all from the collection of Justin Strauss, photography by Nora Scarlett; bottom, The Franklin Mint; pages 130 and 131: all from the collection of Justin Strauss, photography by Nora Scarlett; page 132: top left from the collection of Justin Strauss, photography by Nora Scarlett; courtesy Viewmaster; page 133: courtesy Viewmaster; page 134: courtesy Viewmaster; page 135: all from the collection of Justin Strauss, photography by Nora Scarlett; page 136: Hanna-Barbera; page 137: from the collection of Justin Strauss, photography by Nora Scarlett; page 138: Jordan Reicheck; page 139: top, from the collection of Justin Strauss, photography by Nora Scarlett; middle left, Jordan Reicheck; middle center, Hanna-Barbera; middle right, Hanna-Barbera; bottom left, Jordan Reicheck; bottom middle, from the collection of Justin Strauss, photography by Nora Scarlett; bottom right, Hanna-Barbera; page 140: all from the collection of Justin Strauss, photography by Nora Scarlett; page 141: Capitol Cities/ABC Inc.

ACKNOWLEDGMENTS

The authors wish to thank the many people who were instrumental in helping to put this project together. Despite deadlines, as many convoluted plot twists as Fred and Barney could conjure up, and the Northridge earthquake, the book is a reality; we couldn't have done it without you. Everyone at Hanna-Barbera was wonderful. We would especially like to extend our appreciation to: Bill Hanna and Joe Barbera, invaluable sources of information; and their secretaries, Ginger Robertson and Maggie Roberts; Fred Seibert, Tom Barreca, and Walter Williams for pointing us in the right direction; Iwao Takamoto for sharing his knowledge and his drawings; Jerry Eisenberg for the recollections of times past and his collection of photographs; Scott Miller for his help in obtaining visuals; and Tom Wogatzke for patiently answering endless questions. Others outside the studio were indefatigably helpful, too: Hoyt Curtin for the music; Ed Benedict and Tony Benedict for the memories and insights; Justin Strauss for the wealth of memorabilia and information; Don Garrett and Jeff Rose for the memories—and the laughs; our agent, Mitch Rose, for being there when we need you; our editor, Crawford Barnett, for the long hours and unfailing support. And finally, thanks to all the animators, artists, voices, and production people, present and past, who took the time to give us insight into the prehistoric first family and who, through their special talents, have made the Flintstones a Modern Stone Age phenomenon.

And to the memory of Dick Bickenbach, who answered our myriad questions with laid-back charm. We're glad we got the chance to know him.